OPPORTUNITY OF THE ORDINARY MAN

An Autobiography of a Successful Salesman

BY DEREK HALLING

First published in 2004
Media Sales & Marketing
40 Bishopstone Drive
Brighton BN2 8FF
United Kingdom

British Library Cataloguing in Publication Data.
A catalogue record for this book is available from the British Library.

ISBN 0-9547819-0-2

Typesetting and origination by
Oliver and Graimes Design Associates Ltd.
01273 465411 www.oandg.co.uk

Printed in Great Britain by Ashmore Press, Worthing, UK.

OPPORTUNITY of the ORDINARY MAN

An Autobiography of a Successful Salesman
by **Derek Halling**

PART I

Cape Town, South Africa, 1996. The Rolls Royce had met Françoise and myself at the airport and was transferring us to the luxurious five star Ellerman House Hotel in Bantry Bay. I was totally bewildered by it all. How could it be me in the Rolls Royce? The very ordinary guy from the very ordinary background while it was all those other poor bastards who were living in the tin shacks of the homesteads we were passing. I had the same feelings the previous year in New York city when it was Concorde from Heathrow to JFK, a suite at the Plaza, a great evening of jazz at Fat Tuesdays, a couple of Broadway shows and on to Tokyo. Meetings with Sony and Matsushita, then Samsung and Goldstar in Seoul, Korea before stopping off for a few days at the Mutiara on the beach in Penang, Malaysia and then home to Brighton, England.

Some lifestyle. But why me? Fate? Maybe - but 1950's singer Doris Day and her old song 'Que Sera' really did not convince me. Luck? Sure luck plays its part but it must have needed more than that. All my doing? Could be, but probably not altogether me.

These kinds of thoughts had been nagging for quite awhile. With my nose in a third gin and tonic while overlooking the magnificent Cape Town coastline, I tried to come to some conclusions. It wasn't easy. As I reflected, my mind drifted back some sixty years.

A WELSH MINER AND A SURREY FARM GIRL (1935-1940)

England. 69 Bushey Road, Sutton - previously in the county of Surrey, more recently of Greater London. A pleasant road, I seem to remember, with mainly late 19th century semi-detached houses with elm trees along either side. The trees were regularly trimmed to stop the overhanging branches slapping the big red double decker 156s and 164s as they roared out of the nearby garage at some ridiculously early hour wakening even the hardiest sleepers. The noise of those early morning buses was one of my earliest recollections and our family's only form of transport taking us up to the top of Sutton High Street for shopping or a visit to the Gaumont or Plaza cinema. Or maybe to Morden where we took the underground train for occasional visits to central London - some ten miles away.

Six Bells Coal Mine in Abertillery, South Wales where my father spent years working underground before walking to London looking for work in the recession of the '20s.

Reginald Halling courting Elsie Elizabeth Lawrence (later to become my parents) Circa 1929.

My parents wedding day in Sutton, Surrey surrounded mainly by my mother's family and friends. The cost of travel from Wales to London was simply too much for my father's relatives to attend.

Our family rented the ground floor of number 69 while my father's brother Bill and his family, rented the upstairs. My only living grandparent, Gran Lawrence - my mother's mother - lived two doors away at number 65. So, one way and another, it was quite a family affair.

My father Reginald Halling, originally a Welsh miner, was partially deaf and as a young man had rheumatic fever which left his heart in a generally poor condition - but he never used that as an excuse for not getting things done. He had actually walked from Abertillery, Monmouthshire to London in the late '20s looking for work - he was that sort of man. He stayed with some friends in Sutton for a while before meeting a lovely young lady from a Surrey farming family, Elsie Elizabeth Lawrence. They fell in love, got married and had two wonderful sons - my big brother, Trevor and two years and two months later, Derek John born on 8th August 1935 - and that's me.

NARROW ESCAPES IN THE 'BLITZ' (1941)

Our mother was terrific - so much love and attention. And later when the going got tougher, nothing was too much trouble for her. Like so many Mums, she would starve herself before Trevor and myself needed for anything. But also like so many Mums, she was concerned more with the immediate comforts of her chicks than any longer term plans. I guess with the survival era of World War II, that wasn't a bad thing. That was another of my early recollections - WWII. With his ear glued to our old Philips wireless, I saw my father's face turn pale as he told us that we were at war with Germany. He tried to explain what that meant but, at the age of just four, it was a little difficult for me to grasp. However, within a couple of years, I had learnt fast. It was the height of the German air raids (otherwise known as the 'blitz') over London and I would sneak out of the Anderson air raid shelter in our back garden while my parents were napping and do all sorts of exciting things that kids of those years liked to do - collecting shrapnel (pieces of fragmented metal from the bombs and shells), watching the airplanes go over and so on. But one day, or should I say night, really made me understand what war and life was all about.

Our flat consisted of just three rooms - the front room where we lived, a kitchen/scullery where we cooked, ate, bathed (in an enamel bath), did the washing with the aid of a wood fired copper and the bedroom where all four of us slept. My parents in a double bed with the kids in bunk beds. Of course, Trevor, being the elder, occupied the top bunk.

One particular December evening, two of my aunties, Mollie and Peg, home on leave from the WAAFS (Women's Air Force), were due to pay a social visit. Because of their anticipated late arrival, Trevor and myself were packed off to bed at the usual time. Trevor climbed on to the top bunk as always, but, like kids do, I dived into Mum and Dad's bed, hid under the covers and eventually fell asleep. The aunties, for whatever reason, did not arrive. That meant an earlier than expected bedtime for Mum and Dad. Typical Dad on seeing me in their bed exclaimed,

"Put him in his own bed!"

Typical Mum's reply,

"Oh let him stay with us, poor little soul, he's fast asleep".

Thank goodness Mum won that one. About an hour after we were all sound asleep, without any warning, a German bomb had scored a direct hit on our house. In fact, it passed through the front part of the house and exploded right in the spot where the little social gathering would have been taking place - probably killing everybody. It completely blew away the front part of the house but left the rear part relatively intact. I don't recall the actual explosion but vividly remember waking up and seeing stars where the sidewall should have

been. I also remember hearing the words,

"Where's Trevor? Where's Trevor?"

Trevor was in fact where I should have been - on the lower bunk bed. The supports of the bunk beds had collapsed and Trevor, together with the bed frame and mattress, had

Aunty Peg (left) and Aunty Molly in their WAAF uniforms. They should have visited on the night our house was destroyed by a stray German bomb - with all our family indoors.

That's my big bruvver, Trevor, and me during WWII - well protected, we thought, for anything that may fall out of the sky!

My first introduction to saving money! You could collect penny stamps like this until you filled the card and then exchange them for a one-shilling savings stamp.

dropped about five feet on to what, thankfully for me, was an empty bed! Not one of us had a scratch. Frantic calling out established that everything was OK with our relatives upstairs. Uncle Bill had a not-too-serious cut on his forehead, but aunt Ada and daughter Phyllis were uninjured.

We were all led out of this filth and rubble by the men of the ARP (Air Raid Precaution). One, who turned out to be the father of a great friend-to-be Terry Clarke, who lived in nearby Vicarage Road, carried me out. We were taken to a friend's house where we stayed until Dad found another house to rent in Stayton Road, just across the other side of Sutton Green - a few minutes walk from Bushey Road.

Our family was never particularly religious, but there must have been someone, somewhere watching over us that night.

By the way, if you visit Bushey Road these days, you won't find 69. Gran Lawrences's house at 65 is still there and 67, but then there is a gap and it then jumps to 71. For whatever reason, it just wasn't rebuilt.

FIRST GLIMPSES OF LUXURY AND EVACUATION (1941-1945)

12 Stayton Road was a double fronted house with plenty more space than we had in Bushey Road. In fact, I even had my own bedroom! However, the intense German air raid activity meant that most nights all four of us slept together cramped under one of those heavy-duty steel Morrison table shelters in the dining room.

On reflection, I don't know how we managed financially. Dad had a job as a milk delivery roundsman and Mum did some cleaning work a few mornings a week in a large house in Grove Road - the 'posh' southern part of Sutton. I would go with my Mum to help out during the school holidays and that was a whole new world for me. The lady of the house was rather fat and would always still be in bed when we arrived at about 9.30 am while her husband was out at work - 'something in the City' - whatever that meant. The rooms seemed enormous with rather elegant furniture - so different to our collection of 'utility' pieces mainly given to us after we were bombed out. They even had a car! Also a huge garden with a gardener who came several times a week. All this was my first awakening to lifestyles that, at that time, I didn't know existed.

I had started school, which I took in my stride. It was something that you had to do, but certainly not at the age of five and for many years to come, I didn't fully understand that it led you into what you were going to do for the rest of your life. The fun times at Crown Road infants and junior schools were often interrupted by air raid warnings and when another German bomb fell on a grocery shop just opposite our house in Stayton Road, father decided to move the family to where fewer bombs were dropping - Abertillery in south Wales. Back to his roots and a real adventure for Mother and us kids. We soon got to know many of our father's relatives, most of whose lives had revolved around the coalmines or the pits, as they were locally known. Life was simple for those men of the valleys - leave school at 14 then straight down the pits. That was it. Few seemed to have either the initiative or inclination to break out.

My grandfather and grandmother, on my father's side, were already dead, so we shared the house of uncle Tom and aunt Betty in Arrail Street in Six Bells, a small community just down the valley towards Newport from Abertillery. We were crammed liked sardines with cousins aplenty who made us very welcome but obviously had some resentment of our infringement on their space.

After a few months, when the 'blitz' had quietened down, we returned to Sutton once again only to have a V1 flying bomb (colloquially known as a 'doodlebug') totally demolish Benhill School some 400 yards from our house. Luckily, it was early in the morning around six a.m. that the monster hit, so there were no children in the school. The devastation was pretty severe and the explosion took out every window and door in our house. That was it - back to Wales! This time we shared uncle George and aunt Lou's house in Cyril Place, Old Blaina Road, Abertillery where there were even more cousins! - Clarence, Joyce, Betty, Jack and Mary - all of us sharing three bedrooms. And while we kids enjoyed all the fun, I think the stress must have been a bit much for the adults.

Life in Abertillery was totally different from south London. Trevor and myself walked

Gran Lawrence, a super lady, who defied all the German bombs and stayed in London all through the war.

over two miles to school. There were closer ones, but we wanted to return to the Six Bells School that we attended on our earlier stay in Wales. It was great fun meeting up with our old friends and cousins once again and swapping all the stories about the war so far. We had been bombed out and bombs had fallen all around us - including a doodlebug - whereas the nearest bomb to have dropped in Abertillery was nearly twenty miles away near Cardiff. Trevor and myself were quite celebrities!

Father soon got a job working at the Bulmer's cider factory in Hereford. It wasn't anything special but, according to him, labouring was better than nothing - it keeps some money coming in. And that was the first real lesson I learned about life - keep some money coming in whatever your circumstances.

After a few months in Cyril Place, our family managed to find part of a house in Carlyle Street to rent. I reckon George and Lou and their family were pleased to have the extra space and beds to spread themselves around once again.

Meanwhile, back in Sutton, Gran had been busy. She had stayed in her house throughout the blitz, determined not to let those 'jerries' beat her. She would write regularly keeping us informed what was going on back home. As soon as the war was almost over, she started lobbying Sutton Council Housing Department on our behalf. And magic! - We were allocated a new, nissan hut style house in Beulah Road, Sutton only about a half mile from Bushey Road. So, once again, we packed our bags for the all-day return journey via Newport and Paddington station in central London on the steam trains, and then the underground to Morden and the 156 bus back home in Sutton. Wales had been fine, and certainly safer than London, but it was really nice to be back home again. And even Dad said so...

NEW BEGINNINGS AND JAZZ BANDS (1945-1952)

We settled down again in Sutton quite quickly, just in time to join in the street parties to celebrate the end of the war. Dad again soon found a new job - this time as a building labourer on the new mail sorting office that had been destroyed by yet another German bomb - and Mum was very happy to be back with her Mother and sisters not so far away. Naturally, it was back to school for Trevor and me. I sailed through the 'eleven plus' entrance examination to grammar school. Sutton County had the pleasure of my company for the next five years leading to a half dozen GCE Passes in 1952. School and learning had been relatively easy and

The 4th Mid-Surrey Boys Brigade Band in 1946. They taught me to play trumpet for which I became eternally grateful. By the way, I'm the shortest kid in the band standing next to the tall guy in the back row.

enjoyable for me. English was OK, school French - seven out of ten. Maths was tricky, history quite boring and irrelevant (an opinion I was to change later in life), and geography was very exciting. The state of the big, wider world interested me immensely - even at the age of twelve - and that interest has stayed with me ever since. I always got AAA in music as the teacher 'Spike' Hindle favoured me because I played trumpet in the school symphony orchestra, which he conducted.

Around the age of 12, I had joined the 'Boys Brigade' and learnt to play trumpet in the silver band. I must admit that I wasn't over keen on the twin concepts of 'Discipline & Religion' on which the Boys Brigade was built. But I did enjoy the band. We played at church services, street parades, band contests, concerts - we even played some big venues like the London Albert Hall and the Westminster Central Hall - and I always had my share of solos. It was great fun.

I took the Boys Brigade trumpet to school to play in the school orchestra and several of my class mates, Norman Garner, Arthur James and Johnny Holmes and myself, soon formed an unofficial band playing a bit of jazz and some of the popular tunes of the day. To start with, we only played in the midday breaks at school. But it soon developed into Saturday afternoon rehearsals at Arthur's parents house and later Sunday morning rehearsals at the local Labour Party hall with kind permission of one of our other school friend's father who was a local activist in that particular political party. Meanwhile, Terry Clarke, the son of the guy who had carried me out of the bomb rubble in Bushey Road, had joined the band on piano and we became very good friends - a friendship which has lasted until his death in 2001.

Our first proper 'gig' was at the Sutton Public Hall for a function on behalf of the local prospective labour parliamentary candidate: Our 4-piece band was lost on the vast stage and we were as nervous as hell. Things didn't go that well and we had some complaints. It didn't upset us, as we learnt plenty from that experience and we were all very determined to carry on. The main lesson I learnt was to give the customers what they want - or at least what they think they want. It was not very professional to play the sort of music that the boys in the band wanted to play (like jazz) when most of the paying customers wanted a waltz followed by a foxtrot.

The Sunday morning rehearsals at the local labour hall continued until we were offered a series of dance dates for the Young Conservatives at the Highfield Hall in Carshalton Road, Sutton. Some local Labour Party bigwig

Despite my parents' lack of money, they always gave us kids a good time - like this caravan holiday in Hampshire in 1947.

8

Having learnt to play trumpet, I started doing gigs before I left school. Later, I supplemented my regular day job income quite nicely over many years by playing a couple of evenings each week. This photograph was typical of the gigs in the late '50s. *Left to right:* John Hemmings (trombone), Edgar on bass, 'Mole' Whittall (drums), me on trumpet, Terry Clarke (piano) and Norman Garner (tenor saxophone).

found out about it and immediately stopped the free use of their hall for rehearsals! We were not at all politically driven but simply money and pleasure motivated - we didn't care which party we played for! And this has held true for the rest of my life - I could never identify completely with any of the major political parties. The Socialists or Labour Party seemed totally concerned with sharing out cakes without any understanding that you could not share out anything until it was made in the first place. On the other hand, the Tories or Conservative Party were only concerned with the money making process and keeping as much of it as possible in the hands of the middle and upper classes. They shared no real caring or understanding about ordinary people and the genuinely needy in our society like war widows or those guys who had lost their limbs on the Normandy beaches.

The money we earned on each gig, helped take off the pressure on our not so well off parents in providing pocket money or allowances. Having said that, my parents did everything they could to treat us well with annual holidays to the Isle of Wight or Dorset, weekly trips to the cinema and, for very special occasions, a show in the West End like 'Oklahoma' or a pantomime at the London Palladium.

Another problem - the Boys Brigade found out that I was earning money on gigs by using their trumpet and that they did not like. They took the trumpet away from me and only made it available when I attended rehearsals or 'official' Boys Brigade functions. Fair enough, I thought, and immediately solved the problem by a visit to Selmer's, the Charing Cross Road musical instrument store in central London, and paid a deposit on my first very own trumpet. It cost nine pounds and with my Father's signature on the hire purchase papers as guarantor, they let me take the trumpet home straight away. I paid for it in six monthly installments financed by an early morning paper round and my gigs. I kept that instrument for many, many years and the return on capital was very satisfactory - not that I thought of it quite like that in those days. All I knew was that I enjoyed playing and enjoyed the money and really couldn't enjoy either without a trumpet!

One of the major problems at school and later in life was my inability to do any more work than was needed to get by - just enough study to get through the next test or examination with plenty of last minute swotting. I was always in the top four or five out of a class of around 32 - and to me, that was plenty good enough. It was the same with playing the trumpet. Once I could get on a stage and play well enough to entertain an audience, I stopped improving. I just couldn't see the point in becoming a better player because I had already done enough to achieve my goal of playing well enough to send the audience home happy. Trevor, my brother, on the other hand, had played euphonium in the Boys Brigade and had later taken up the trombone after which he simply wanted to be the best trombonist in the world. He later became a fine big band player and was a full-time professional for a few years with the Harry Leader Band and George Crow and His Blue Mariners. This was before the arrival of rock and roll, which saw the bottom fall out of the market for dance band trombonists. For me, I kept my day job and continued doing gigs in the evenings for additional income. We had a very talented guitar player in the band during that era and when rock and roll came in, he could play all the great riffs of the day. The guitarist was Vic Flick who later left our band to join a band called the 'John Barry Seven'. John Barry went on to write much of the music for the 'James Bond' movies and Vic is the main man you hear on all those great hits. We did not have a singer in the band at that time so I was the one to learn some Elvis Presley and Little Richard numbers to become a not-very-good but passable rock singer!

Stay flexible, move with the times, keep your eyes open and watch out for new opportunities...these were my thoughts at the time. To this day, I am not sure who was right - Trevor for being a perfectionist or me as the realist.

THE WORLD OF PHILIPS ELECTRICAL (1952-1959)

With my father's health deteriorating and having to pay regular visits to St. Helier Hospital in Rose Hill, Carshalton, where he was ultimately to die, money in the family became more and more of a problem. Neither parent ever said that I shouldn't go on to advanced education or university, but it was clear that it would be very difficult financially for me to do so. So I made a decision to leave school and start a career. But what? I didn't have a clue. Whilst my father lacked any real commercial experience, he seemed to have an earthy grasp of the ways of the world. "Electronics, my son," he pronounced. "Electronics is the way ahead and you could do worse than getting involved." That was pretty shrewd of him, considering that transistors had not yet been invented and TV hadn't taken off in the way it did in the UK after the Queen's coronation in 1953. So that's what I did - wrote many letters, attended dozens of interviews and at the age of 17 was eventually offered a job as a trainee with Philips Electrical in their service department on Purley Way, Croydon at a starting salary of three pounds and seventeen shillings per week. My first task was repairing bicycle dynamos but quickly moved on to Philishave electric shavers, tape recorders, radio and TV. I worked hard and thus progressed very rapidly. Philips allowed us one full day a week at the local adult education college in order to study for our technical qualifications. In addition, I voluntarily attended three evening classes each week. So what with gigs and evening classes, there wasn't too much time for regular girl friends - just the occasional date. I was growing up fast and having a good time. I was learning a trade and earning enough to pay Mum a reasonable contribution towards the housekeeping money. The gig money paid for clothes and some beers with the boys. Life was good.

TWO YEARS FOR QUEEN & COUNTRY (1953-1955)

One cloud on the horizon - National Service at the age of 18. This meant two years in the military whether you liked it or not - and for me, not. The thought of being trained to kill disturbed me immensely and to be paid just over £1 per week for the privilege, was a not-very-funny joke. A near 65% pay cut compared with my job at Philips!

There were some complicated ways of avoiding National Service, but in the end, decided to go along and make the best of it. And that is exactly what I have been doing with my life ever since - making the best of situations, grabbing the opportunities that have presented themselves and always making things turn out for the better.

One thought that occurred to me around that time was the fact that the military provided all the basics like room, bed, uniforms and food - at no charge. Was this an opportunity to save some money despite the apparent low pay? Yes. I made a decision to live on £1 per week and save anything I earned over the pound. The pay went up after six months, so again I drew only the £1 and had the army automatically put the balance in a savings account. Doing the same again when the pay went up after 12 and 18 months meant I finished my two years with over £100 in the bank. And that was quite a considerable sum for a working lad in the '50s.

So after just over a year at Philips, on 23 November 1953, 22938789 Private D. J. Halling, found himself on a freezing parade ground at the REME (Royal Electrical & Mechanical Engineers) training camp in Blandford, Dorset being screamed at by some neckless deformee who, I believe, was a drill sergeant. I just didn't know what had hit me! Drill, jabs, kit and dick inspections, serious physical exercise, lousy food, bromide-laced tea, no music, firing guns - it was all nearly too much, but I survived.

There was one saving grace - as soon as the basic 'square bashing' was finished, I was allocated a place on the Telecommunications Mechanic course starting at Arborfield in Berkshire. And that would make a very positive contribution to further my chosen career both at that time and in the future.

Four months trade training at Arborfield, near Reading in Berkshire was, by comparison, a holiday camp. All day studying - both theory and practical work - followed by fun evenings in the NAAFI drinking pints of bitter with your mates or a visit to the camp cinema to see the latest Diana Dors movie. We were allowed to go home every weekend (about 25 miles by train or hitch hiking) on a 36 or 48-hour pass. This meant we could see our families and friends before returning to camp late on a Sunday evening to start studying again on Monday morning. No parades, no inspections, no real bullshit - life was acceptable. That was until a snap inspection called one Monday morning established that my belt was not of the required level of cleanliness, so I was punished with five days jankers! For the uninitiated, that meant five days confined to barracks with all sorts of parades, inspections and additional duties like scrubbing the toilets or the cookhouse floor. As it happened, things did not turn out too badly for me. The duty sergeant lined up all the 'prisoners' outside the guardhouse ready for inspection by the duty officer. I was standing closest to the sergeant and while we were waiting for the duty officer to arrive, I heard a sweet nothing in my ear:

"Where yer from soldier?"

"Sutton, Serge," I mumbled.

"Where the bleeding 'ell is Sutton, soldier?"

"Near Croydon, Serge."

"Croydon eh? Then you must be one of Derek Bentley's and Chris Craig's boys right?" (Convicted robber/murderers from Croydon)

I didn't actually say yes but didn't exactly deny it either. I just sort of half smiled. Every other soldier was told to report to their respective place of menial chores but I was told to report to the guardroom and put the kettle on! I spent most of my five days making and drinking tea with this wonderful bull-like sergeant chatting about whether Derek should have gone to the gallows or not and how lucky Chris was to still be alive considering he was the one to actually pull the trigger and kill the policeman.

"Another mug of tea, Serge?" And from then on it was, "Have a nice weekend soldier" as I passed him at the camp gate on the way home.

Aged 19, stationed with REME in Duisburg, Germany fixing radio transceivers most of the time (but also occasional guard duties!)

Things were looking up even more as our course neared its completion. Each course of 16 participants was allocated 16 postings and the guy who finished top of the course could have his choice of postings, the second guy his choice and so on. Our crew was allocated postings in Korea (mopping up after the war), Egypt, Germany, Ashford, Kent and Mill Hill in northwest London. As I finished third on the course there was still a choice of any of the postings. I didn't fancy Korea or Egypt too much but thought it would be nice to see some other part of the world, so I plumped for Germany. By the spring of '54, I found myself in Duisburg, Germany. Not particularly the most attractive city in Germany but a place that was to play a significant part in my life.

FUN TIMES IN DUISBURG, GERMANY (1954-1955)

We were the 87th Tels. Workshop, REME (Royal Electrical and Mechanical Engineers) - a small support unit of around 30 men based in the largish Glamorgan Barracks together with an armoured battalion and the Army Catering Corps training school for BAOR (British Army of the Rhine). Apart from the wicked pollution from a nearby chemical works that belched heavier-than-air pungent yellow fumes all over the barracks from time to time plus really not enough work to do, life was bearable.

We were supposed to repair the radio transceivers installed in troop carriers and tanks but we did not find many in need of our skills. We went out on exercise only once in eighteen months to the Minden area but saw no real excitement. As part of this non-action, life became fairly routine including spasmodic weekend duties from time-to-time to answer the phone that never rang. Taffy Launder and myself were on duty in the orderly room this particular Sunday afternoon reading the '*News of the World*' and drinking tea, when we saw two girls stroll by the other side of the chicken-wire perimeter fence just two or three yards from the orderly room window.

"Look-you, boyo, crumpet!" yelled Taffy.

"Yeah, so what?" was my enthusiastic reply.

"Give them a whistle boyo!"

"You give them a bloody whistle"

"I can't whistle!"

So I obligingly shoved my head out of the window and gave them a whistle. The girls walked on a few paces then stopped.

"Get out there and chat them up, boyo!" Taffy screamed.

"You get out there and chat them up."

"I can't speak German."

"I can't speak bloody German either!"

So we compromised and both went out to chat them up. I guess we would have been in trouble had the phone rang and nobody was there to answer it. Standing orders quite clearly stated that 'the phone must be manned at all times'. But with the prospect of girlie company at the age of 19, sod it, who cared?

The two girls spoke reasonable English and we made a date to meet up as a foursome the following evening. Anita was my date and Taffy teamed up with Waltraud. Waltraud was somewhat overweight had a typically dominant German personality - but Taffy did not seem to mind. Anita was sweet. Quite pretty with a lovely personality and we were to see each other a lot over the following months. We even met up in England when I was on leave and she was visiting some relatives in London. I introduced her to my parents who thought she was wonderful. It all fell apart shortly afterwards but meanwhile she had introduced me to a male friend of hers Wolfgang. Wolfgang played guitar and invited me to join his band on trumpet and vocals. We became good friends and spent most weekends at his parent's home in Beek, a suburb of Duisburg about 10 km from Glamorgan Barracks. His parents almost adopted me as their own. They were fantastic. They fed me, found a bed anytime I wanted it and generally made such a fuss of me. The band played mainly for fun and occasionally money. At that time I was trying to learn the language and German songs. 'Oh, Mein Papa' - made famous by British trumpeter Eddie Calvert in the U.K. was always a popular number when it was my turn to play a solo. With Hans, Nico and the other boys in the band plus a collection of nice young frauleins always hanging around, we really had a great time.

I managed to live well on my £1 per week. The British pound was worth 12 marks in 1954 and a meal of schnitzel, kartoffeln, gemuse plus a few beers in one of the local German pubs would cost about 3 marks. I didn't smoke at that time (in fact, I have never smoked), so I bought my weekly ration of seven packs of 20 cigarettes at one shilling per pack and sold them to the Germans at one mark per pack (or one shilling and eight pence). A handsome mark-up of 66%! One of my other non-smoking friends, somewhat less enterprising, couldn't be bothered to do the same. I would buy his ration too and make an extra four shillings and six pence. With these small-time 'black market' fiddles, I managed to increase my weekly allowance by almost 50%, which meant from time to time we could visit one of the rather expensive jazz nightspots in Duisburg or Dusseldorf. One of the most enjoyable days in my life, in fact, was when I managed to see and hear my hero Louis Armstrong live for the first time. A concert at the Rhein Halle in Dusseldorf that featured the all-stars with 'Satchmo', Trummy Young, Barney Bigard et al, was simply sensational. On to a late nightspot to listen to an excellent local modern jazz trio of piano, bass and drums, completed a perfect day.

But with time now passing quite quickly, November '55 soon came round. And the thing which had occupied my mind for so much in the early days - demob - didn't seem so important with so much fun and many nice people around in Duisburg. But it was 'Auf Wiedersehen' to all my German friends and back to Sutton on the train from Duisburg to the Hook of Holland for a troop ship to Harwich followed by the train journey to Aldershot for final demobilisation. After a few days of formalities, I was a free man once again! Not yet 21 but two years of 'duty' which, to start with, I had dreaded, had made me into a happy, confident young man ready to face the world with some fresh ideas about life in general and over £100 in the bank! I had certainly made the most of that opportunity.

PART II

OUT OF SERVICE INTO SELLING (1955-1959)

By the time I was out of the Army, Trevor had already finished his national service in the RAF. Mum and Dad were so pleased to have us around once again. Trevor had perfected his trombone playing in the services and was now playing professionally. He had also met his future wife, Patricia, and things were already looking serious between them. Their future seemed settled.

But for me, it was back to Philips in Croydon... and I was already having some doubts about the wisdom of remaining a service engineer for the rest of my working life. I rationalised things to myself like this: the only reason most people worked at all was in order to make money. Some people talked about 'job satisfaction' but that doesn't pay the bills. I admittedly enjoyed the work at Philips but found out that the guys who had been with the firm for 40 years or more, were earning only a couple of pounds a week more than me - which was depressing. Things were really brought home when one of my middle-aged work mates told me he was going into hospital the next day for a simple hernia operation. The poor devil never came back - he died under the anaesthetic. I asked myself what had he achieved with his life? No doubt he had been a good husband and father and had always made a living - but clearly not much of one. Did he really feel satisfied with his life? I doubt it. I worked harder than most of the other guys in the workshop but got paid just about the same. My mind was coming around to the simple concept of being rewarded directly according to the effort made. Payment by results - call it what you will - it simply means the harder you work, the more you get paid - with no upper limits. And those thoughts were very exciting.

During 1957, I had a semi-regular girlfriend called June, whom I had met at a dance in Cheam Hall, in Cheam Village - not very far from the flat in Farnham Court where my parents had moved into while I was in the army. June and I enjoyed each others company very much but we had not thought about anything more important than about which movie was on at the Granada next week or which jazz band was playing at the Queen Victoria pub, North Cheam on Sunday evening. Marriage, houses and babies were a million miles from my mind and I think hers too - but how quickly things were to change. Not with June though - it was another lady that came into my life called Sieglinde. It happened like this:

Wolfgang and myself had kept in touch with each other since I left Germany and I had an open invitation to visit and stay with them at any time I wanted. It was in September 1957 that Norman Garner and myself decided to have a week's vacation and we reviewed our options. Some of the boys were off camping in Cornwall, others to Butlin's Holiday Camp in Bognor, but we decided to visit Wolfgang in Germany. Earlier in the year I had bought a Lambretta motor scooter, which was to be our fun means of getting to

Germany. We made reservations for ourselves and the scooter on a flight with Channel Air Bridge that flew from Southend Airport in Essex to Rotterdam in Holland. The flights were on old converted Bristol Freighters, which carried 3 or 4 cars and a few motorcycles and scooters. The carrier on my scooter was stacked high with Norman's tenor saxophone and clarinet, my trumpet and two suitcases full of clothes, and off we set. I was a little nervous about meeting up with Wolfgang and his family again. But I need not have worried! As we turned the corner into where they lived, we saw a massive banner stretched right across the street saying 'WELCOME BACK DEREK!' and suddenly we were surrounded by Wolfgang plus all the Plein family and many of the neighbours too, giving us the most magnificent welcome one could ever have expected. Frau Plein cooked us a wonderful meal while Herr Plein kept the Koenig Pils and his favourite schnapps flowing.

The whole week was packed with parties, visits to the steel works, more parties, jam sessions, more parties and so on. We hardly slept a wink - but who cared? Wolfgang had a very large 'small black book' from where he seemed to be able to pull girls out of the hat just whenever he wanted.

We were due to travel back to England on Friday 13 September - unlucky for some - and so a final evening was arranged for Thursday. Wolfgang had invited three girls to join us to go on a recording session with some of his local musician friends. One of the girls was Gisela and the other two were sisters, Sieglinde and Walburg - all very attractive young ladies who lived in the area. For some reason, the recording session was cancelled at the last minute - so we all went off to Charlie's Bar for the evening. I really don't know the reason, but I did find myself talking to Sieglinde more than the others and at the end of the evening, she and I exchanged addresses. Overnight, I developed the flu and felt terrible the next morning. Poor old Norman had to do all the driving back across Holland to Rotterdam and when our Bristol Freighter revved it's engines and took off, I thought I was about to die. Four hours later, I was at home tucked up in bed with a hot water bottle. Gradually my temperature went down and it was back to work on Monday.

A few days later, a post card arrived for me. Guess who? Right - Sieglinde or Sigi as most people called her. I wrote back and things stayed that way like pen friends until some months later a letter arrived from Wolfgang saying he would like to visit us in England during the summer and bring two friends with him. Could we find accommodation for them? No problem there. My parents agreed, as did Norman's. Who were his friends? Well, they were girls of course - another little beauty called Ursula and who would believe it? Yes, Sigi. The three of them stayed for a month and Norman and myself reserved a cabin cruiser on the Norfolk Broads for a week during that time. Norman fancied Ursula and, naturally, Sigi and myself paired off. For one brief moment, I felt sorry for Wolfgang. He was sort of going to be alone. I needn't have worried -

Wolfgang was the master of the pick-up. He even jumped from our boat on to another one passing in the opposite direction because of a bevy of bikini-clad maidens he had spied on board. We simply tied up down stream, then waited a couple of hours for Wolfgang to come trudging back along the towpath!

It was the end of the month and time to say goodbye. Wolfgang was ready to get back into his own routine once again and Norman and Ursula were ready to say Auf Wiedersehen but Sigi and me? I don't know…we just did not seem to want to part. We talked over the various options of me living in Germany or her coming to England. My German was not good enough to work in Germany - so that was out of the question. (It was only some 18 years later that I found out about the English-speaking markets in Germany primarily the U.S. military market which was eventually to be my making.) As far as Sigi was concerned, she would be happy to come to England but her father had recently pulled a few strings to get her a good job in a laboratory, and she knew to refuse would upset him. However, to cut a long story short, Sigi arrived in England to work as a nursing auxiliary. We were to get engaged Christmas 1959 and married in the following September.

THE DEXION ERA (1959-1962)

My thoughts regarding work at Philips and the future now had to be balanced against Sigi's ideas of how life should proceed. To say the least, she was conservative and unimaginative. Safety first, seemed to be her motto. I suppose you could say that as love had blinded me somewhat, I tried to please her in every way possible. However, I did make a few big decisions which affected our lives against her wishes and the first of which was to leave the world of service and get into sales. She wanted me to stay in the security of a big organisation but after thinking of Fred, my friend who died, I was soon working for Dexion as a territory salesman. Dexion made storage systems for all types of commerce and industry and what a great training they gave me! The first thing I learnt was how the ability to 'sell' didn't simply mean that you could be a salesman on the road. It also meant that you could influence others in all aspects of life like politics, convincing your bank manager to extend your overdraft or even just helping the family make up its mind where the annual holiday should be taken this year. The ability to plan and prepare all the necessary information and present it in a credible, plausible way to whomever is a very important skill for every person to have.

The next thing Dexion taught me was how untrue the old adage of 'the best salesmen are born not made' was - they taught me everything. All of the theory of selling including the building of a presentation - attention, interest, conviction, desire, close - as well as the importance of planning, pre-call preparation and meticulous record keeping. They explained to me all about 'buying motives' or the reason people buy things - greed, profit, vanity, status, pride, efficiency etc - and taught me how to assess the person or persons you were pitching and establish in your mind their most likely buying motives, and then how to modify your presentation accordingly. It was all completely new to me and totally absorbing.

Over the years, I have heard many definitions of a 'sale' - but I like Dexion's the best:

'An exchange of goods or services, usually for money, to the mutual satisfaction of both parties'. The emphasis must be on the word 'mutual'. Selling is not ramming down the throat something that someone does not really want. It is the process of the salesman satisfying the needs (sometimes hidden) of the buyer and both feeling good about the deal they have done.

And, of course, we had total immersion in the company, their products and their applications. The training was both initial and continuous, classroom and field based. The motivation from management was superb and I was bursting with enthusiasm by the time I went 'on the road' for the very first time.

My first sales territory was London SE1 which contained a wide variety of large organisations like Guys Hospital and Gonzalez Byass (wine importers) plus hundreds of medium sized firms who could benefit from my products. Most of the work was cold calling - which was a great initiation - with an occasional lead from an outfit that had made an enquiry through the office. I soon started getting orders and I enjoyed the work immensely. Since those early days, I have been eternally grateful to Dexion for taking a raw, inexperienced but enthusiastic recruit and turning him into a professional salesman.

I earned some big commission payments on top of a higher base salary than I had earned at Philips, but Sigi hated it. She loved the satisfaction of knowing where I was at all times of the day - punching the clock at Philips just before 8am and then doing it again just after 5.30pm. Now it was erratic hours, an idea she just did not like at all. In vain, I tried to explain that the harder I worked, the more sales visits I made and the more money I earned for us.

SAD FAMILY TIMES (1959-1962)

Our official 1959 Christmas time engagement was totally overshadowed by the death of my Dad only a few days earlier. We said goodbye as we buried him on Christmas Eve in Sutton Cemetery and spent the rest of the holiday feeling generally miserable but at the same time, trying to console Mum. To make matters worst, she just did not like Sigi and Sigi did not like her. The tensions between them were bad and they became only marginally better as our wedding day approached the following September. We arranged to get married in Duisburg with a civil ceremony and church service on 5th September. We chose a Monday because my father-in-law-to-be said we could use the pub, which he had built a few years earlier for the reception as it was normally closed on Mondays. He and I got on well and I just loved my mother-in-law and Sigi's sister and her two younger brothers. My mother and Sigi's family smiled at each other a lot and tried hard to communicate - but it was very tricky.

Again tragedy struck just at the wrong time. Trevor, who couldn't get the time off work to come to Germany for the wedding, sent a telegram that arrived the day after the wedding day. We thought it was another message of congratulations, but we were totally shattered as we read that Gran had died instantly after stepping off the pavement directly into the path of a car on the day before our wedding. The train and ferry trip back to England was brought forward as the funeral had been arranged quite quickly. Once it was all over, we settled down to our new lives - but the next big shock was just around the corner - we discovered Mum had cancer.

On reflection, it seems the only thing that my new wife and I had in common was our readiness to be parents. We agreed to have a baby straight away and would live on the money I would earn. In other words, I would be the breadwinner and catch the rabbits while she would cook them and be the traditional homemaker.

I had enough savings to put down a deposit on a new smallish bungalow on the coast in the Saltdean area of Brighton and after spending a couple of weeks at my Mum's house, followed by a month or so in a furnished flat, we moved into our new home. Things were looking up but Mum's illness overshadowed our lives. She had always wanted a little girl but only had two boys. She then started looking forward to a grand daughter - Trevor and Pat had just one kid - Nicholas James. Then it was our turn and we were already expecting our first. In those days, you did not know the sex of your baby in advance and when Martin William was born in June 1961, we were over the moon but Mum was a little sad. She dearly loved baby Martin but was still hoping for a little girl in the family. Mum's treatment was ongoing and she would be in and out of

hospital over the next year or so. We were pregnant again and that cheered up Mum no end. I told her it would be a girl this time and I was right. The only problem was that my mother died just a couple of weeks before our beautiful daughter Andrea was born. That was hard to bear. Probably not the worst thing that

Mum and Dad in our house in Collingwood Road, Sutton shortly before Dad was to die in 1959.

ever happened to anyone but pretty damn close. To lose your Dad, Mum and only living grandparent within two years at times which should have been moments of great joy and celebration was, to say the least, tough.

Trying to turn those events into something positive was difficult. The best I could come up with was not to take yourself too seriously as you never knew what was around the corner. I formed the attitude that you were born and one day, sooner or later, you would die. Achieve whatever you could in between, and make life as pleasant and rewarding as possible for yourself, those around you and, wherever and however, the rest of humanity.

I stayed with Dexion for around three years and then made some changes - some bad and some good. It was tough having a wife who couldn't or wouldn't morally support me and seemed to resent everything I did and blamed me when anything went wrong. However, in the early days, she did a good job in taking care of the kids and I got on earning a living in the best way I knew how - selling plus a few gigs.

KEEPING THE MONEY COMING IN (1963)

One of the bad times came when the firm I had joined, just three months earlier, went belly up on 1st December '63. It was known as the 'Bedding Guild' made up of 12 small divan bed manufacturers, which were trying to compete with the 'Slumberlands' of this world by pooling their resources and each making a bed to the same specification, calling it 'Rhapsody' and advertising the product on national TV. It was a nice idea in concept but ultimately poorly executed with quality control a major problem. The sales force sold-in well, but once the merchandise arrived in the furniture stores, the buyers soon lost confidence due to a general lack of quality in both the materials and workmanship when compared to competitive models at the same price point. The 'Bedding Guild' could not agree a salvage plan and decided to close the whole operation down. We all lost our jobs without notice and received very little severance pay.

Luckily, I had three or four well-paid gigs lined up for the week before Christmas and New Year's Eve. I started sending off applications for a proper job but needed some instant daytime work to supplement the gig money. I found temporary work for the Post Office pulling mailbags full of Christmas cards and parcels off the trains at Brighton station. It was heavy work and we worked shifts - which was ideal for me as I could work the 6am to 2pm shift, go home, see the kids, eat and get ready for the gig. I would arrive home from the gig around 1am, catch a few hours sleep and be back humping those bloody mail bags again at 6am. But as my Dad had told me all those years before, "Whatever you do, keep some money coming in!" And that is exactly what I was doing.

I also had to fit in the job interviews and just after Christmas, had been offered a position with Thomas Hedley, the U.K. industrial foods division of the mighty

U.S. Corporation, Procter & Gamble. P&G had an excellent worldwide reputation for sales and marketing training and had been used by many as a passport to key jobs with another organisation a few years down the road. You can find P&G-trained executives in just about every commercial and industrial organisation throughout the world.

For me, it was a hard one to call. On one hand, I needed a job and I had been offered a job - with a good base salary. On the other hand, there was no commission whatsoever. So my concept of payment by results would be totally out of the window.

DOING IT THE PROCTER & GAMBLE WAY (1963-1969)

For reasons I have never fully understood, salesmen in the U.S. are rewarded mainly by commission and few perks but in the U.K., basic salaries plus company cars and free BUPA (health insurance) seem to dominate. And that's the way it was with P&G U.K. Anyway, I took the job. It was selling fats and margarines to bakeries in SE England - a completely new world for me. The training was totally field based and consisted of one week with a trainer and then one week on your own. Another week with the trainer and another week on your own followed by a final week with the trainer. After that, it was up to you and your area sales manager. Things started badly and then went rapidly down hill from there.

The major problem was that P&G were rigid disciplinarians and my trainer was a robotic nut case. On our first meeting, we had a somewhat surreal conversation, which went something like:

"Do you wear a hat?" he asked.

"No," I responded, "I never wear a hat."

"All P&G salesmen wear hats, and you are now a P&G salesman, so you will wear a hat," he instructed me.

"But I don't own a hat."

"Then go and buy one."

"But I don't have enough money to buy a hat."

"That is no excuse - go and buy a hat!"

So I went and bought a hat - a dark grey trilby that perched uncomfortably on the top of my head. I was totally unfamiliar with handling a hat - especially in a bakery environment, as I was soon to find out.

The training was parrot fashion stuff - nothing like the outstanding professional sales training I had received at Dexion.

"Listen," my trainer would say, "I will tell you this only once. Then you will do the next call and present it to the baker exactly like I presented it to you."

The fact I knew nothing about the baking industry meant that, when the baker asked me a question in the middle of the pitch, I couldn't answer it in any way, shape or form. And my trainer would simply stand there and say nothing. When we were back in the car, he would tear me apart and criticise my performance. I pleaded for some basic knowledge of the industry and the basic concepts of baking, but no - "This is P&G and this is the way we do it."

I struggled through the first few days, which were totally humiliating. I even considered resigning there and then. Things came to a head when I was giving a parrot fashion pitch to some working bakers in a small back street bakery in Norwood, south London. They knew that I didn't know what I was talking about and started poking fun at me. One of them, without me noticing, took a huge whisk full of wet sponge batter and bounced it on the floor right next to me, splattering penny-size blobs of muck all over my dark suit, brief case and newly purchased trilby hat which I had placed on a work table nearby! I almost burst into tears but simply collected my sales aids, put on my filthy hat, said "f*** you lot!" and walked out. I refused to talk to the trainer, so he drove us to the regional office in Pall Mall, central London and left me sitting in the car while he disappeared to consult the regional manager. From both sides, it was pretty close of whether I stayed or whether I went. I stayed and decided this was another opportunity that I just had to turn to my advantage.

The fundamental problem with P&G was that selling soaps and detergents like 'Camay' and 'Ariel' to the consumer via supermarkets had achieved all their huge successes. Big TV campaigns and massive couponing promotions would determine the 'flavour of the month' and the salesman would simply walk into the buyer's office with a pre-planned order and tell the buyer this is what he would be shipped. Product knowledge was not important - only how fast the goods would move off the shelves.

The industrial foods division was relatively new and all of their training programmes were based on their retail activities. At that stage, they had not fully realised that there is a big difference between selling to a store manager or buyer who is purchasing to resell directly to the consumer and selling to a craftsman who is going to incorporate your product into some other product before adding value and selling it to the consumer or end user. The baker needed to know that you knew what you were talking about before he would take you seriously. And that was my challenge. I gave lip service only to the P&G way and performed according to the book when my area sales manager worked a day in the field with me. But meanwhile, read up everything I could about the industry and got one or two friendly bakers to spend some time with me and learnt from them whatever I could - the jargon, common practices, what was going on with the local trade associations, what my competitors were up to and so on. At weekends, I would work with some of them in their bakeries actually making cakes and getting to know exactly how things worked. P&G knew nothing of this! My confidence was now totally restored and while selling 'flavour of the month' when my area manager was with me, I was doing it my way as soon as his back was turned. Their approach was the old fashioned, pushy-pushy way without rational thought, which has given selling a bad image over the years. In my opinion, my approach was the truly professional way - intelligent, planned, and fully considerate of your customer's needs and not just your own. So having survived those initial traumas at P&G, I was now schitzo!

Putting my new plans into action was great fun and very satisfying. My largest potential account was Duncan Foster in Eastbourne who had about 50 retail bakery shops around Sussex. Instead of walking in to see the production manager on my monthly journey with my 'flavour of the month' sheet and saying, "Good Morning Mr Baker, I'm here to demonstrate SUNCUP cake margarine, and him replying, "Oh not you again, you know I don't buy anything from Procter & Gamble, I walked in and said, "Why don't you sell cream slices in your shops?"

"How do you know we don't sell cream slices?"

"Because I've visited nearly all of your shops and can't find a cream slice anywhere. You must know that Marks and Spencers sell a lot of cream slices - it seems you may be missing out on something here."

"Well, I must admit, we have tried cream slices some time ago but we couldn't get the right quality and costings to be able to compete."

"I think I may be able to come up with something that may interest you. Give me a day or so and I will be back."

I went away, did some checking and came up with a formula using one of P&G pastry margarines that gave him just the right quality and just the right costings for him to be able to compete with M&S. I went back the next day, (I had to break my rigid journey cycle to do it) showed him the formula, went through the costings and suggested to him that I send him a minimum order of four 28 lb cases of CRISBAK pastry margarine for a trial production run. To this he agreed. The four cases were duly delivered and the trial took place. Test tastings were carried out and the results were very positive. The next thing I knew was that cream slices were going into full production and he placed an order with me for TWO TON of CRISBAK - 160 cases! This one order took care of my CRISBAK target for almost a whole year! What's more, when I walked into his office next time around, his opening remark was, "Hi Derek, pleased to see you.... the cream slices are selling really well - please rush me ANOTHER two ton of CRISBAK!

That's the way to do it I thought, and repeated this approach with many other accounts over the next year or so. Of course, by this time, the figures were talking for themselves and I was breaking all sorts of sales records.

There was only one drawback - no commission. Plenty of glory, but you can't pay the bills with glory. Too many U.K. based salesmen seem obsessed with basic salary and status symbols such as cars. The perks such as company cars and expenses seem to cloud their total thinking and limit their real total earnings potential. If you ask them for the reason, they mumble on about "the security of a high basic salary if business is bad" and "It's nice to have a company car because you don't have to pay the bills to get it fixed". They seem to ignore the fact that they will probably get the sack if business is bad. I was once chatting to a print salesman who handled huge volumes of business for his company. If he only had one or two percent commission, he would have been earning big, big money. But he told me that he preferred a higher basic salary with no commission, as it was easier to borrow more money to finance his home! I couldn't believe it! Here was someone who preferred to borrow money and pay dearly for it - rather than to earn it himself and not have to borrow it in the first place!

A LOVE AFFAIR WITH BRIGHTON & HOVE ALBION (1963 - TILL I DIE)

It was during my time at Procter & Gamble that I found another big passion in my life - Brighton & Hove Albion Football Club - later to be nicknamed "The Seagulls". My Dad had taken Trevor and myself to see some of the big London teams like Chelsea, Arsenal and even Crystal Palace in the late '40s when I was about 12 years old. The crowds were huge. I remember walking out of Chelsea's ground at Stamford Bridge when the crowd was so dense that I could take both feet off the ground but was still carried along! We all watched the Stanley Mathews cup final on TV in 1953 but I hadn't really developed a big interest in football. It was Easter 1963 when my father-in-law was paying us a visit from Germany and we were deciding what to do for entertainment over the bank holiday weekend that it happened. I suggested horse racing but he asked if there were any football matches going on in Brighton. Despite having lived in the place for a couple of years, I didn't even know if Brighton had a professional football club. I checked the newspaper and found that Brighton did have a team and they were playing that very afternoon at home to Bournemouth. I asked my neighbour if he knew where the stadium was and he gave me directions to the (later to become defunct) Goldstone Ground - the home of Brighton & Hove Albion. Willi and myself stood in the North Stand to watch Brighton lose 0-1. The club was even relegated that season to the old division four - but I was hooked. I have been worshipping at the alter of the blue and white stripes ever since. Through ups and downs - mainly downs - I have been a devoted fan. Of course, like father like son. Martin became a Brighton fan when he was seven. Likewise Colin, our third child to be born in 1970, who today into his thirties, has been watching Brighton for well over 20 years. Even my daughter Andy watched Brighton for a couple of seasons. I found out that it was Neil Smillie's legs that attracted her! I suppose he was one of the more glamourous players around at that time. He played quite well too.

FIRST STEPS IN MANAGEMENT (1968)

Back to P&G... My excellent sales performance, as I have already said, was attracting a great deal of attention. My performance was so good that I was appointed Sales Trainer for the region. This meant I still retained responsibility for my sales territory but had to implement the training of any new salesmen joining the company in our region. Now this left me in a real dilemma. I still hadn't come clean with my area or regional manager - they thought I was achieving bumper sales by good old P&G methods! And now they were asking me to train others! Should I train the new guys in the P&G way or my way? That was the question. I eventually made the decision to do everything that P&G training manual told me to do but superimpose at least a smattering of my ways - and it worked and it worked well. Two new guys were successfully trained and performing well which meant Derek Halling was in the spotlight once again. This time it was promotion to Field Assistant. I was to give up responsibility for my sales territory and concentrate on 'management'. It was a six-month assignment to see whether you were ready for the first steps into management.

I attended high-level meetings at the U.K. Newcastle-upon-Tyne H.Q. and got to know top management more than just names and faces at annual national sales meetings. At this point, I decided to come clean. I reasoned they were not likely to fire me having just promoted me. It worked... I explained my ideas with the knowledge that my sales territory had seen 100% plus increases annually for the previous two years against a national average of around just 10%. As part of my time as Field Assistant, I rewrote much of the Sales Training Manual incorporating many of my ideas to create a much more professional way of selling. And that was very satisfying...believe me.

It was also during this era, that I learnt a great deal about the wider subject of marketing. How selling was just one of the functions of marketing along with market research, product development, sales promotion, advertising etc. As well as

After breaking all sales records at Procter & Gamble, I had my first taste of man management having been promoted to area sales manager for Northern Home Counties. This photograph shows me and my team receiving the first of several awards from George Poulton, the general manager of the industrial foods division in 1966.

reading everything I could on the subject, I was able to talk to and pick the brains of many of the P&G brand managers and advertising agency people to broaden my knowledge and experience.

After six months, I was promoted to Area Sales Manager for Home Counties North and had my very first experience of man management. I had a mixed bunch team of seven with which to contend - some old-timers and some raw recruits - and found it exciting and thoroughly rewarding. My pay cheques were now substantially higher than before but I soon confirmed what I already knew - an experienced P&G manager could command a far higher salary elsewhere. So after a total six years with P&G, I decided to move on. It was to be Osram-GEC, the lamps and lighting manufacturers.

THE ARNOLD WEINSTOCK YEARS (1968-1971)

I loved the new job with Osram. I was an area manager with a team of some twelve guys consisting of retail salesmen, salesmen selling to architects and designers plus technical lighting engineers. I had to study hard to absorb a lot of new product knowledge and industry know-how to have and hold the credibility of my subordinates. I did and it worked. Business was good but under the Arnold Weinstock regimes of the late sixties, GEC was in a constant state of change. I could not believe some of the reorganizations that took place or the speed at which they happened. The fastest was just two weeks.

On a Saturday in September 1969, the whole Osram sales and marketing organisation was summoned to a meeting at the Royal Lancaster Hotel on Bayswater in central London where a complete new structure was announced. It was exactly two weeks later around 9 o'clock in the morning that I received a call at home to change everything once again. I answered the phone:

"Derek Halling speaking"

"Hello Derek, this is Bill Morgan" (a name I knew only vaguely in the company) "and I'm your new boss."

"Good morning Boss"

"And you are one of my new divisional managers"

"Is that good?"

"It means you've still got a job"

"That's good"

"Had you planned to be in the office on Monday?"

"Do you want me in the office on Monday?"

"Yes"

"Then I will be in the office on Monday"

Monday morning came, and once again I drove the tiresome journey from Canewdon in Essex where we lived to the Osram offices in Wembley, Middlesex to get the full story of what was happening. Bill explained he had been appointed National Sales Manager and ordered by the board of directors to slash the size of the sales force by 50%. I couldn't believe it. Just two weeks earlier this was to be the great new way ahead and now, my old boss had gone and within another two weeks, some sixty salesmen together with two whole levels of management would go. Some of my co-area managers had already been let go and my job was to combine two of the old areas of twelve men each thus having to lose twelve of them within the next few days. It was a tough task to fire some excellent people who had been with the company for years and who had previously personally told me how proud they were to be part of such a great company as GEC.

But as there was nothing I could do, it certainly taught me a lesson. A lesson of how to work hard and professionally but NEVER put your total faith in any company or organisation. At 33 years of age, I made a few promises to myself that day. Firstly, there was no way I wanted to be working for any one else by the time I was 50. It was such a tragedy to see a 40-something-year-old married man with kids still at school who had worked for the same company since he left school himself, lose his job for no real reason other than the next quarters profit forecast was looking weak. My next promise was to become as financially secure as possible as soon as possible and never to be wholly dependent on needing the next pay check to meet the monthly mortgage payment and to keep the bank overdraft down to reasonable limits. With a demanding wife and hungry kids to feed, that one was not easy, but I did manage to build up our net asset worth quite considerably over the next decade and become very much more financially independent.

Getting back to Osram. I was a part of the new structure for only a short period of time. I had done my job and fired all those mostly good guys and I spent the next couple of months trying to convince those who still had a job that they would keep it. I felt so two faced - not having any real control over those matters, I nevertheless had to try to motivate the team to achieve our targets and must have done a pretty good job because I was invited by the board to become National Sales Manager for a subsidiary company, Ascot Lamps & Lighting. Unlike Osram, which was a highly promoted, high-end brand, the Ascot product was a secondary brand that depended much more on price. A small team of more entrepreneurial-minded salesmen doing big volume, lower profit deals was totally new concept for me and a great new experience. It was my first national job involving sales trips as far apart as Scotland and Jersey, which meant more nights away from home and more hassle from the wife.

Despite the hefty pay raise and my personal satisfaction of the promotion, she could find nothing to enjoy about it, only complain. The wife (or 'spouse' or 'partner' due to PC ideology language of today) factor plays a far bigger part in moneymaking or career progression than most 'experts' would ever care to think about or dare write about. I was beginning to think that there was no way I could make this woman happy. She failed to grasp the basic situation that everything has a price. She wanted new clothes, new cars, holidays, new houses, new furniture but thought I should be able to provide all these things from the few pounds each week I had earned at Philips when getting home at six each evening. I would try to explain the impossibility of that scenario and tell her the choice was hers - the simple life with low income or a more exotic lifestyle that had to be paid for by work. And the higher your position and income, the more time you would be away from the family. Each day, my mind would fill with thoughts about her total lack of understanding of the realities of life, which tended to depress me. But I never allowed them to jeopardise my work performance.

GIN AND JAGS IN CRANLEIGH (1969-1974)

We eventually sold the house in Canewdon and moved to Cranleigh. It was a pleasant Georgian-styled house on the edge of the centre of this leafy small town deep in the gin and jag belt of the Surrey countryside. We had great neighbours in Cranleigh - Alan and Jan McCall next door, Kath and Betty next door but one, Brenda and Bas Jervis and Gerry and Barbara Haine lived opposite with Peter and Maureen Turner just down the street. We never lived in each other's pockets but would get together for an occasional party or to go to a Cleo Laine and Johnny Dankworth concert and we have met up regularly ever since. Most of us have moved on but get back together in Cranleigh every New Years Eve for a great party. Despite living in Germany or Bahrain or wherever, we all have always made it back for our annual bash. It started in 1972 and is still going strong in 2003.

Colin, our third child, was born in Cranleigh in 1970, which was another wonderful event in my life - this time fortunately not marred by some family tragedy. At the time, Martin was nine and Andrea eight and were developing extremely well and participating in all the usual activities of kids of that age. I spent all my spare time with them having fun, taking them away on holiday and other trips and generally encouraging them to do good things. My marriage started to look shaky but there was no way I was going to walk out on those kids. I had, and still have, a simple philosophy about marriage - if two people come together through choice then they can separate through choice. But if, as a result of that coming together, there are children, then that changes everything. Both parents must ignore their own frustrations and feelings by focusing solely on the needs of the children. I was determined to be a full time father until all three kids could stand on their own two feet as sensible, well balanced adults.

I was headhunted away from GEC with a very, very attractive offer to join an old established timber and sheet material importer with their head office and main depot just south of London Bridge. A personable second-generation 47-year-old businessman ran the organisation, employing around 80 people. With trade in the doldrums, he had fired a few of the old timers and employed a few whiz kids in an attempt to revitalize things. A sharp accountant and myself as an equally sharp sales and marketing man, were to be the answer to all their problems. But unfortunately it did not work out that way. Before we could put our plans into action and give them time to work, the boss had realised he was sitting on real estate worth millions of pounds. The founders of the business, his father and uncle, had purchased the freehold of not only the London Bridge site, but also three other depots in Surrey and Sussex. One day, after deciding to have them valued, he found out to his surprise that they were worth millions more than he thought. There and then, he sold up. The value of the business was not huge but he was to live in luxurious retirement on the proceeds of the sale of the property. Despite the fact that I was out of work after only six months, I couldn't help but admire his decision and if I had been in his shoes would have done exactly the same.

Back then to writing letters, visiting the recruitment consultants, talking to old contacts - anything to get another job quickly. I filled in by selling photocopiers for a while before landing a position with the Sperry Rand Corporation. I was to be National Field Sales Manager for the Remington Consumer Products Division whose main product was the Remington shaver. I couldn't help smiling to myself as I was offered the job - one day Philips Philishave, the next Remington! What goes round comes round....

Another substantially higher pay cheque, a large company car, a rather grand personal office in a tower block in New Malden near Kingston-on-Thames and a great job in charge of an eighteen strong sales force through three regional sales managers.

CORPORATE LADDER CLIMBING - REMINGTON STYLE (1971-1976)

As corporate life goes, Remington was as good as it gets. Locally medium sized but part of a large international group, which was successful and well respected. The management team, highly professional, included some great personalities like Northampton based, distribution manager, Rudi Kluz and advertising manager, Rod Wheeler. It was definitely a work hard/play hard environment where the only real motive was to get the job done. That is a long-lost concept in so many companies today, where only internal politics, backstabbing and survival for long enough to be able to cash in your share options seem to prevail.

The Remington sales force was particularly well trained and motivated, so I didn't have to make any drastic changes when I took over. One of the three regional managers seemed to resent my arrival. But a man-to-man chat between us soon established that he was thinking of making a move - our chat simply speeded up the process. I decided to give a young Aberdeen based salesman, Nigel Bryden, his chance of first line management by asking him to take over the Northern Region as soon as the other guy left. Nigel flourished and I guess he felt exactly the way I did when I got my foot on the management ladder at P&G just a few years earlier. He joined Maurice Franks (midlands) and Kevin Wearn (south) to form a formidable regional management team

I simply had to reinforce the basic rules of management - selection, training (both initial and continuous), motivation and control. I then had to set up just a couple of new rules. The main one being 'total honesty' - no cheating, no skiving, no lies, no bullshit - and it all worked really well.

For me, personally, the commute from Cranleigh to New Malden was much easier and after a routine day in the office, I would return home earlier than before but still my wife wasn't happy. When I was about to take a trip it was something like - "Oh here we go again - you staying in all the best hotels and eating in all those fancy restaurants while I'm stuck at home eating peanut butter sandwiches with the kids. This was totally unfair and unreasonable as Remington were one of the top companies in involving wives wherever and whenever possible. She, in fact, attended all the major conferences and social activities in London and Paris and also accompanied me on a seven-day incentive visit to New York. I really do not know what she had to complain about - but complain she did.

After just one year, a few changes happened at Remington that meant promotion for me. Bryan Nicholson, the then managing director of the U.K.

The Remington UK management team circa 1975. From left to right: Rod Wheeler (advertising), Cyril Edmunds (service), Mike Grafton (finance), myself (sales and marketing) Rudi Kluz (distribution) and MD Brian Spencer (seated). Corporate life at Remington was as good as it gets.

operation, resigned to join Rank Xerox and later become top-man at the Royal Mail. He was, and probably still is, a clever man and I really started to develop my management skills under his influence. Brian Spencer, my immediate boss, the general sales and marketing manager got the top job and he in turn, moved me up into his old position. That meant more money, more people, and more responsibilities. Things were looking good but I simply could not escape from certain thoughts. Thoughts along the lines that despite an uncooperative wife, if I was capable of achieving what I was achieving now, how much more could be achieved with a supportive, understanding wife?

I guess the main problem in that area lies in the fact that many people probably get entangled with a marriage partner before they are sufficiently mature in themselves in knowing what is important. Also what we, as individuals, are looking for in life. All the emotion, the sex and the excitement of togetherness of the early days of a relationship, tends to overshadow the hard, practical everyday situations that occur later. Love, one feels at the time, will conquer all. But it is only after some years into a marriage with a few babies around, that you find out the true differences between you and your spouse. It would probably be far easier if you had to sit some sort of compatibility test before commitment - but I suppose the romantics would not be in favour of that suggestion for one moment!

I found out the strength of a good marriage second time around, but that is a story that came later.

My first marriage came to its first major crisis when I arrived home in Cranleigh after a long drive from Manchester around 11pm to find the three kids fast asleep in bed but with no signs of their mother. I went ballistic. She showed up some 45 minutes later and did not really have any sensible excuse. We had previously agreed that we would never leave the kids alone, day or certainly not night. It came to light she had been out playing around and not for the first time either. I should have walked out there and then but I simply could not and would not leave the kids - especially now that I knew her attitudes of responsibility towards them had deteriorated. Maybe I should have left and taken the kids with me - but how could I? With such a demanding job, that was impossible. From then on, any night I had to spend away from home meant that I was constantly concerned that my 11, 10 and 3 year olds were alone in the house while she was out and about.

We sort of weathered the storm for a while and, on the odd occasion, actually communicated sensibly without screaming or shouting at each other. One thing that came out of our talks was that despite the fact that we made regular trips to see her family, she seemed to be homesick for Germany and that maybe we should start to think about living in Germany. My immediate reaction was that this could be the way to make this woman happy. But how wrong I was to be....

PROPERTY BOOM AND SLUMP (1972-1974)

During 1972 and 1973, U.K. house prices had shot up at unprecedented levels with the result that our house in Charts Close, Cranleigh had tripled in value over five years. This prompted some shortsighted folk to buy even bigger and more luxurious houses in the Surrey hills by borrowing even more. Those involved were let down badly when the property market slumped in 1974 and they moved into negative equity. I knew several families who lost their jobs and could not afford to keep up their mortgage payments. At the same time, they could not sell their house at a price, which would cover the outstanding debt.

I took totally the opposite attitude and made one of the biggest and best decisions in my life. On the simple concept that you will always need a roof over your head and that there will always be the worries of keeping a job to ensure meeting the monthly mortgage payments, I saw this as a big opportunity to create some real financial stability in our lives. I totally ignored all the middle class twittering and constant pressures of the 4-oven aga brigade to move, what they called 'upwards and onwards' by borrowing even more money, and started to look for a much cheaper home. Not necessarily a smaller house, not necessarily one in the wilderness - but a cheaper home come what may. I eventually found a house back in the Saltdean area of Brighton, which was exactly what I was looking for. A nice position overlooking the sea with the same number of rooms as our house in Cranleigh. It was convenient for schools and shopping and still commuterable to New Malden. The best part was that it was run down and in need of renovation. An old lady had lived in the house for years without doing any modernisation. She had died and the heirs were eager to dispose of the place - so the asking price was low. I made a silly offer then eventually negotiated a price, which enabled me not to require a mortgage. At the age of 38, it was a very nice feeling.

My wife went along with it all without too much bother and generally we regarded it as putting our recent problems behind us by making a fresh start. We also agreed that at some time should we move to Germany, it would be easier to let a house on the coastal strip of Brighton, than inland in Surrey. I was determined to keep a bolthole in England, wherever we would go and whatever was to happen.

The amount saved out of my monthly pay check by not having to meet any mortgage payments, soon paid for the renovations and refurbishment to make this new house an attractive and comfortable home. And for the first time in my married life, I (or we, I suppose I should say) had a positive net asset worth - the value of what we owned was worth more than what we owed. And as anyone who knows anything about anything - that is the only test of how well you are doing.

ACCOUNTANTS IN TOP JOBS? NEVER....

Remington was moving along nicely. Obviously, my primary job was to build profitable sales by motivating the sales force and ensuring the key account managers were taking good care of the Boots and Currys of this world. My other responsibilities included above and below the line advertising and promotional activities, coordinating with distribution colleagues to ensure enough product was available from the factories in France and Austria and of course, the preparation of profit plans. This was the beginning of an era of my dislike of 'bean counters' - that wonderful breed of corporate accountants who think they know everything when in actual fact the only thing they know is how to count beans. Actually, Mike Grafton, the Remington U.K. controller and company secretary at that time, was clearly one of the good guys. But some of the European H.Q. specimens and certainly those from across the big pond in Bridgeport, Connecticut and Park Avenue, N.Y. were highly suspicious.

Why is it, my argument would go, do company accountants think that revenues or turnover just appear from nowhere? Why don't they understand that somebody, somewhere has to sell somebody something and get paid for it before anything happens and they can start counting the beans? The consumer has to be sold by effective advertising while the wholesalers and retailers have to be persuaded to stock your brand. These things take time and cost money.

Company accountants can only see the cost side of the profit and loss account. They always think they can cut cost without affecting the revenues. It is an easy way to have an instant increase in profit but so often they don't realise that the cost they wish to slash is the salary and expenses of a key account salesman responsible for millions of dollars worth of revenue. Or cut a major TV advertising campaign that is totally necessary to maintain market share against some vicious competition. One of the biggest business problems of the last decade of the 20th century was that corporate accountants called far too many of the top shots - and these trends seems to be getting worse in the 21st century. The 'WorldCom' and 'Enron' scandals in 2002 exposed some of the bad guys and highlighted many of the problems. Accountants have always demanded an instant return on capital with only the short-term interests in mind of share or stock price. They simply have never been trained or even begin to understand about generating or creating business like the marketing and sales professionals do. They do not understand market trends, market research or how consumer tastes can change. Do they know what customer service really means? Their breadth of knowledge and experience is usually insufficient for them to fill the top jobs. The accountants should be there simply to support the business creators. Innovative products like the Sony Walkman would have failed to leave the ground if the decision was left to an accountant. He (or she) would have probably demanded some previous historical data of a similar product project before giving the final OK. Only a marketing visionary like Akihito Morita and his non-financial team of professionals knew this product would make a lot of money for Sony and change the whole face of the consumer electronics industry. Accountants simply do not have an insight in these matters. They only know about what they see on a piece of paper or a computer screen.

Another good example of the moneymen making bad decisions took place during my time at Remington. Remington had introduced the first electric shaver to the world in the 1930s. It had a hard flat head with slots and underneath the head it had cutters that vibrated back and forth to remove the whiskers from your face. Compared with wet shaving, it was much more convenient. Getting back into full production after WWII, Remington made giant strides in converting wet razor users to dry electric shaving. Other major manufacturers like my old firm, Philips, Braun of Germany and Ronson in the UK, noticed this market growth.

Philips launched their first Philishave that used a new rotary technology. It was a single head model which consumer research showed was not as efficient in removing whiskers as the Remington shaver but was far more comfortable. If you wanted, you could run a Philishave over your face for hours with no bad effects. On the other hand, if you had a slightly sensitive skin and over-used the Remington, you would become slightly sore with blotchy patches on your face. It was generally agreed, by those trying to be objective, that a shaver combining the cutting efficiency of the Remington and the comfort of the Philishave would be a market winner. Enter the foil-head electric shaver. These shavers changed the head technology again by using an ultra thin, flexible foil stretched over steel cutters in a curved shape. German electrical giant Braun put plenty of their muscle behind their new shavers in continental Europe and started taking market share - mainly from Remington. Braun stayed out of the UK for some years and left the launch of foil-head shavers to Ronson under some little understood agreement.

Market research showed that consumers in direct comparisons preferred the new foil heads than with Remington and Philishave models. They seemed to be efficient and comfortable. But the Remington top brass (mainly moneymen) simply did not want to know. They saw it as a 'selling' problem. "Get out there and sell harder", they would say when attending our management or sales meetings on their visits from the U.S. They simply didn't even want to consider the thought that maybe the old pre-war production facilities in the U.S.A and France for making slot head shavers were becoming obsolete and ignored the facts that some new investment might be necessary.

Eventually, under severe pressure from the non-moneymen, we were given the go-ahead to launch a foil-head shaver in Europe. It was to be branded the Remington F2 but would not be made by Remington. It would be sourced from Payer, an Austrian manufacturer, and was to prove an excellent product. On launch, trade customers in the UK told us: "That's the best shaver Remington has ever made!" We were limited by top management as to the quantities we could purchase from Payer and also forbidden to spend one penny on advertising or promoting the F2! We were directed to spend our advertising dollars on the 'flagship' Selectro slot-head models thereby promoting out-of-date technology and thus continuing to lose market share. It would be the same today if Sony, for example, spent all their money on promoting analogue cassette players while all their rivals were pushing hard on the very latest digital CD or DVD players. It just did not make sense.

I believe the Remington problem was solved after I had left the company and Victor Kiam had bought it from Sperry Rand. As the new Remington commercials would have had us believe, I don't think Victor Kiam really liked the shaver very much but he did realise the tremendous strength of the Remington brand that could be exploited in so many other product categories.

THE DIRTY HAT BAND (1972)

After moving house from Brighton to Canewdon in Essex when with Procter & Gamble during the late '60s, my trumpet playing activities were severely curtailed. But while at Remington, I was to make a come back.

I had received a phone call from an old banjo-playing friend from my days at Philips, Johnny Allen, telling me he had formed a jazz band called "The Dirty Hat Band". Great name I thought. They needed a trumpet player and was I interested? We all got together for a blow and talked things over. It wasn't going to be anything too intensive - once a month in a pub in Battersea and an occasional gig as they came along. That suited me fine when considering my Remington commitments. It was a fun band playing only Louis Armstrong, Kenny Ball and Acker Bilk styled happy jazz.

The pub in Battersea was a bit rough with a few nasty looking types drinking heavily. The landlord told us that fights often broke out but never when we played there. I think we entertained them pretty well. I was the front man and got them singing and clapping along and that kept their minds off more aggressive activities.

Another guy we got singing along was actually in prison. The "Dirty Hat Band" had been asked to play a Sunday afternoon concert in Wandsworth Prison - a place full of murderers, rapists and men with GBH records.

No money, but Johnny Allen accepted the gig. We just did not know what to expect and for only the second time in my musical career, I was nervous. We set up in this huge hall that was used as a chapel and would seat about 600 inmates. We were ready to start playing but there was not yet an audience. Suddenly two doors at the back of the hall opened and in filed the men filling the seats in strict order from front row to the back. They sat there with arms folded, staring straight at us, without a glimmer of a smile from any of them. We were petrified but managed to struggle through the opening number after which there was just a very, very faint ripple of applause - and still no smiles on any of their faces. As front man, it was my job to announce the numbers and I walked up to the microphone that, as I started to speak, shrieked with a bit of feedback. The vicar, who had organised the concert, was also in charge of the PA system. He got up from his chair, on the side of the stage but in full view of the audience, to adjust the volume of the amplifier. Still standing at the mike, I made the casual remark, "Try it in one of the other holes please," and then quickly added, "As the actress said to the vicar!" That was it - the audience fell about with laughter and from then on, the band could do no wrong.

We played and sang the next number which was greeted with very much louder applause from our newly won over audience. Again, I walked up to the mike and said something like, "The trouble with this band, as you have just heard, is that none of us can really sing. Can any of you guys sing? We badly need a singer." With that, a little guy in the fourth row jumped up and shouted, "Yeah, I can sing, I can sing!" He came running up the steps on to the stage with about the ten warders looking on nervously. I shook his hand, asked him his name and what he wanted to sing and we all did a very passable version of 'Bye, Bye, Blackbird'. He went back to his seat with the whole audience cheering, stamping and shouting. A twenty-minute drum solo followed by a rousing version of 'When the Saints Go Marching In' brought our two-hour show to an end.

The inmates just did not want to leave. They just stood there clapping, cheering and shouting for more. All the boys in the band were totally exhausted after the show but Charlie, the clarinettist remarked, "That's the best gig I've ever done - no money, but what a great gig!"

Talking to a trusty who was helping us to pack up the gear after the concert, I remarked that I suppose the guys are so starved of entertainment, that they will applaud anything. "Don't you believe it mate. We get some bands in this place who just come in, play what they want to play and go home. You guys were terrific. You connected with them - you talked to them and got them involved."

A few months later we did another memorable gig - this time at an orphanage for 14 and 15 year olds. Most of the kid's parents, we were told, had been killed in car and other accidents. And that was an even tougher audience than Wandsworth Prison to win over. Who ever heard of 14 and 15 year olds liking jazz? We did it by a very impromptu 'History of Jazz' - you know the sort of thing: "It all started in Africa" - with our drummer desperately trying to imitate the sound of jungle drums. "And the slaves were chained and shipped to New Orleans where they were so sad, they sang the blues." - and into 'Birth of the Blues'.

After that we couldn't remember what next happened to jazz, so we turned to pantomime style humour -

"We're better than the Bay City Rollers!"

"Oh no you're not!" they screamed back.

"Oh yes we are!" the seven of us screamed back even louder.

The kids just loved it all! One of them even came up to us after the show and remarked that he never knew jazz could be so much fun.

These gigs taught me that it doesn't matter how good your product is, it won't sell itself. You must utilise all your communication and presentation skills if you want to get acceptance. Storage systems, electric shavers, jazz band performances - it really doesn't matter, they still have to be sold. Selling is the absolute keyword in making any project successful.

3-DAY WORKING WEEKS (1975)

During my time at Remington, life, for many, in the U.K. was in turmoil. Edward Heath's Conservative government was challenging the old order of union strength. The coal mining industry, encouraged by union leader Arthur Scargill, was constantly striking, which in turn caused coal shortages in the electricity generating industry. This meant random power cuts in the home and a three-day working week in commerce and industry. We could go to the office in New Malden for five days each week as usual but we were not allowed to switch on the lights or use any electricity for two of those days! I would arrive home from work, and settle down with the kids to watch some TV when POW! - All the lights and the TV would go off. The power cuts, petrol shortages, some hoarding of food supplies and so on, caused an air of uncertainty in the country and certainly made me consider more seriously the option of the family living in Germany.

I had been watching the situation vacant ads in the '*International Herald Tribune*' and the '*Frankfurter Allgemeine Zeitung*' (generally regarded as the best German newspaper for job ads) for a few months. By sheer coincidence, just a couple of weeks before a planned visit to Germany, primarily for the kids to see their grand parents, an interesting job ad appeared. It went something like this:

"Sales Executive needed for English-speaking publishing house based near Frankfurt central Germany. Apply in writing to Box..."

I showed it to my wife who, naturally, was very enthusiastic about me applying. I sent a rather short, direct-to-the-point letter, which in simple language said, "I'm a great salesman; if you would like to talk to me, I will be contactable in Germany on the following telephone number from this date to that date." I attached a 'recently taken' photograph; air mailed it to Frankfurt and really did not expect to get a response.

We arrived in Germany, settled down for a relaxing time and a few days into the break I was enjoying a quiet Koenig Pils with Willi, my father-in-law in his local village pub when the door burst open. It was Martin, my eldest, with the news that I had received a phone message from a certain Mr Judd French and would I return his call. I did and the rest, as they say, is history.

I was invited to visit the offices of Overseas Life Verlags GmbH to meet with Judd French in a small German town called Friedrichsdorf, about 25 miles north of Frankfurt. This was the beginning of a whole new world for me - the U.S. Military Market. The market is there due to the worldwide U.S. military presence in countries as diverse as Okinawa, Japan and Iceland. In Europe, the biggest concentration of troops was in Germany with the Rhein Main area around Frankfurt and Wiesbaden being the most densely populated.

In 1976, there were over 320,000 active U.S. military in Europe. Add on their spouses, children, DOD (Department of Defense) civilians such as teachers etc and you had a market of nearly 700,000. The demographics showed that approximately 60% of the GIs were in the 18 - 24 age group and predominantly single. Like most young and single people, they had high levels of disposable or discretionary income. But, unlike their civilian counterparts, they did not have to find money for food, working clothes, or keeping a roof over their head. Everything earned, could be spent on whatever they wanted. In certain product categories like hi-fi or cars, the per capita spend was extremely high. These levels of expenditure attracted the attention of many of the major manufacturers and, as part of their total marketing plans, needed and wanted to advertise to this potential market.

Problem: - with most GIs unable to speak or even understand German, how did you reach them with your advertising message? There was one TV channel - *AFNTV (American Forces Network)* and one radio station, *AFN*. But both were not permitted to accept advertising. The same situation existed with the only specialist military daily newspaper - *'Stars & Stripes'* - no advertising.

Some entrepreneurial publishers had filled this need and at the time I was talking to Judd French, there were some six monthly military magazines and one bi-monthly being distributed in Europe with a further three or four in the Pacific area.

Judd French was the owner/publisher of *'Overseas Life'* - one of the monthlies. He was looking for an advertising salesman for Germany. It was a well-produced general interest magazine running a poor second to the market leader general interest magazine - *'Off Duty'*. Judd French had earlier worked for *'Off Duty'* and its publisher, Walter Rios, but had broken away to start his own magazine because, like so many others in life, thought he could do it better.

Despite only one TV channel being available to the GIs in Germany, there were three monthly TV guides - *'AFN TV Guide'*, *'R&R'* and *'O'Seas Post'* plus a small-ad magazine, which also ran the *AFNTV* schedules called *'Shoppers Bi Weekly News'*.

Judd French explained all this to me during the three hours or so that we were together. He was a tall, softly spoken American some five years older than me. Very likable, easy to talk to and get along with. He was born in Connecticut, USA and had artistic skills having sung and danced on Broadway before turning to journalism. His friend, Stanley, was an operatic tenor who had been offered a ten-year contract with the Frankfurt Opera House. And that's what brought them to Germany in the first place.

I liked what I saw and liked what I heard. When offered the job, I had no hesitation in accepting. My only reservation was the thought that I would not be able to watch Brighton & Hove Albion regularly! But I devised some devious plans to overcome even that objection.

Despite being 'just a salesmen' as opposed to the grand titled position I was currently holding with Remington, my guaranteed income would be over 50% higher plus commission, expenses and a company car. The challenge was exciting.... and, in addition, I thought that at last I would make a certain woman happy by living in the country of her birth. How wrong I was to be on that one...

PART III

WORKING WITH AMERICANS, GERMANS AND A SOUTH AFRICAN (1976)

After giving notice to Remington, we started planning for the big move. Martin, my eldest, at the age of 15 was the trickiest of the family to be considered. He was coming up for GCE 'O' Levels - those critical exams that determined so much your likely future. Martin, himself, had suggested that he should stay in England to finish his 'O' Levels, and then come to Germany a year later. We found him a nice family to stay with in England - a policeman and his wife who was the son of Martin's German teacher at school. Andrea, then aged 14, made a few of the usual teenagers remarks about her friends being in England and why should we go to Germany at all, but really didn't mind too much. Colin, age six, had started school at the Saltdean Primary School but had no problems about our new adventure to Germany. They all knew Germany reasonably well due to the relatively frequent visits to their grandparents and cousins but could not speak the language very well. But how quickly they would learn!

I felt relaxed about everything primarily because we had no massive monthly mortgage payments to find on our home. If I had, I simply wouldn't have taken the risk of giving up a relatively secure job with an excellent global organisation like Sperry Remington for a move to a foreign country to work for a small time set up in what was a whole new market for me. What's more, a few phone calls to local rental agencies in Brighton established we could make another very adequate amount of money by letting our house while we were away. We would rent a home in Germany and the rental income in England would cover that cost. At the back of my mind, I felt totally secure in the fact that, should the whole thing flounder, we could always come back and live in our fully paid up home in England. That gave me the confidence to thoroughly throw myself into making this whole new opportunity really work. Sigi and myself agreed that we would try Germany for a trial period of three years and then review our options.

On 16 May 1976, I flew alone from London to Frankfurt to be met at the airport by the editor of the magazine Bruce Thorstadt - a super nice guy and talented writer. We arrived at the office and Judd introduced me to the rest of the team - Françoise Hauck (girl Friday), Elisabeth Harth (bookkeeper) and Rudi Christ (distribution). Françoise was South African, Elisabeth and Rudi were German and I was to be the first Brit on the team. After the parochialism of much of the UK scene, it was refreshing to be involved in something so internationally wide. I was to find out that dozens of different nationalities worked in the U.S. military markets, including not only Americans but also Japanese, Korean, German, Dutch, French, Irish and even a few Chinese. All with one thing on their mind - making money.

My first night in Germany was spent at a small local hotel where I sampled a few of the local brew and ate a tasty schnitzel before retiring to bed and immersing myself under one of those huge feather duvets that were widely used in Germany at the time. A dreamless night and back to my new office, in my new company car, to start the second day of my new life. The main event of the day was that a larger-than-life American walked into my office and introduced himself as Alan Wingerter. He was the guy who had been doing my job but had been enticed away to work for one of the competitive magazines - '*AFN TV Guide*'. Alan's selling style was typically American - very bold, very brash and almost too positive. But seeing most of the clients were American, his style was very acceptable. Everything was very amicable between Judd and Alan, so Alan had agreed to stay on for two weeks to introduce me to a few key clients and generally familiarise me with some of the quirks of the market.

In 1976, the major retailer to the U.S. military worldwide was AAFES (Army Air Force Exchange Service). Its headquarters was in Dallas, Texas, USA with a European HQ in Munich, Germany. It was by far the largest outfit and sold just about everything from toothpaste to hi-fi and cars through dozens of retail stores known as PXs (Post Exchanges) or BXs (Base Exchanges). Fresh food and groceries were sold by the separate commissary system and NAVRESSO did the same as AAFES but for navy clientele. Alcoholic drinks were sold by the glass through the military club system and by the bottle via Class VI liquor stores.

In hi-fi/audio/photo products, AAFES had a major competitor at that time - the Audio/Photo Clubs. These were originally started by a couple of air force officers who found they could not purchase high-end audio products in AAFES stores. They started negotiating with suppliers to buy say, twenty amplifiers for themselves and their buddies, eventually developing their operation to open around 29 retail outlets all over Europe. The Audio/Photo Clubs were a part of the local military community. Any excess profits after running costs, were ploughed back directly into local MWR (Morale, Recreation & Welfare) funds financing better community facilities such as bowling alleys or golf courses. AAFES also contributed to MWR funds, but this was done on a global basis through Dallas and Washington consequently slowing down the whole process.

AAFES was, and still is, a huge retailer by any standards - in the same league as Sears, Wal-Mart or K-Mart. However, being a quasi-military organisation headed up by a military general, it tended to be somewhat slow and bureaucratic. Stateside, they had to compete directly with the aforementioned store groups but overseas, things were different. GIs were not enthusiastic about shopping off base in a German or Japanese store and maybe having problems with the language. Prices were generally considerably lower on-base where low mark-up and duty free was the order of the day. Every GI on his or her way to a posting from America to Europe or the Pacific would come with a shopping list of must buys on recommendation from an older brother or even a father or uncle. This almost always included some hi-fi, a camera, a watch and often a car for use overseas that could be shipped back home at the end of the tour. Folklore has it that GIs taking them home from Germany generated a big interest amongst their families and friends created the immense popularity of the Volkswagen 'Beetle' in the US.

I found the market to be very entrepreneurial - unlike the more rigid large-company set-ups I had been used to in the UK. Specialist military brokers or rep companies, urged manufacturers to let them represent their sales and promotional interests in the market. These brokers would bang on the doors of AAFES, the NAVY or the Clubs and get orders that would be passed back to the manufacturers for delivery. In most cases, the manufacturers would invoice AAFES and pay the broker a commission. The percentage varied depending on the type of merchandise and the negotiating skills of the broker when setting up the original deal with the manufacturer. Most advertising budgets were controlled by the manufacturers themselves but would not commit to any particular publication unless their military rep company approved. So it was extremely important for military space salesmen to maintain good contact and relationships with the rep companies - even though they would often never get an order from them directly.

COMMISSION ONLY SPACE SALESMEN

On the media side of the market, all of the major magazines mentioned earlier had at least two or three very professional advertising salesmen. Some had basic salaries, company car etc but most were on commission only. They would get at least 15% of the net - but sometimes even more. These guys would do just about anything to get an order and make themselves mucho money in the process! They could make themselves $1500 for selling a single page in a single issue. I knew several young salesmen who were earning over $100,000 - and that was back in the '70s! The equivalent guy back in the UK at that time was on maybe £5000 (about $8000) a year basic with little or no commission plus maybe a Vauxhall Cavalier.

The typical military market space salesman's sales pitch was simple and went something like this: "Our magazine has something for everyone - men, women, teenagers, little kids - it is the simply the best in the market. So buy an ad!" It was a simple approach that worked in quite a few cases. Up until my arrival at 'Overseas Life' magazine, it had been Judd and Alan's approach too. But after a few weeks of familiarisation, I was to make some fundamental changes that had a fairly immediate effect of raising advertising revenues to the highest levels since Judd had started the magazine a few years earlier.

I took the marketing approach, rather than the pure selling approach that all the competitive publishers and advertising salesmen were using. A simple analysis of Department of Defense published military demographic figures, established that while there were over 100,000 married active GIs with their families in Europe, there were over 200,000 single active GIs. All the other publications did a good job in addressing that family audience but none paid too much attention to the needs of the young, single GI. Not much further research soon established the interests of the young, single soldier. Guess what? Right - sex, drugs and rock'n'roll. Add a dash of sport, and that was about it. The more up-market approach of *'Off Duty'* magazine was going way over the heads of your average american soldier - especially as many of them needed help in even signing their own name. During the late seventies, recruitment officers lowered their standards quite considerably to fill their quotas of recruits - hence the not-too-well educated military around that time. It was a scary thought for many of us that the same guys who were handling the nuclear warheads, couldn't even read!

We at *'Overseas Life'* considered all these facts and decided to relaunch as the magazine dedicated to that sector with the highest level of disposable income - the young, single GI. We left the furniture, dog food, ladies underwear and real estate advertising budgets and the like to *'Off Duty'*, *'R&R'*, *'AFN TV Guide'*, *'Family'*, *'O'Seas Post'* and started to amount more serious attacks on the hi-fi, sports gear, beer, cigarettes, travel and entertainment budgets.

One serious problem - we had to sell advertising to survive at *'Overseas Life'*. Like all the other military magazines, it was free-of-charge to the reader. We had to get permission from the local military community commander to distribute our magazine in his facilities. Consequently, any magazine not coming up to what he regarded as some sort of standard was not given authority to be distributed. This meant that a skin book, or a book which enhanced the drug culture, was totally out of the question.

'HUSTLER', 'PENTHOUSE' AND 'PLAYBOY'

Bruce Thorstadt was about to go back to the States. His successor, Bob Cullen and his new assistant editor, James Kitfield, had the tricky job of finding an editorial balance between lively, attractive content which appealed to our young, male readers but at all times tasteful in the eyes of the hypocritical American military authorities. Hypocritical because top-selling magazines in the U.S. included *'Hustler'*, *'Penthouse'* and *'Playboy'* but it would never be admitted by top military brass that their young soldiers ever looked at them! Actually, those magazines were available in the 'Stars & Stripes' military bookstores in Europe but were always on the top shelf enclosed in plain brown paper wrappers! Sales figures for all paid-for magazines were not good as the overseas-based military person had become so used to the proliferation of freebie titles.

Bob Cullen and his wife were offered excellent jobs back in the U.S. and left

Germany. James Kitfield, around 22 years old at the time, took over as editor and did a fantastic job. He identified completely with our audience and understood their needs exactly. He wrote most of the articles, acted as art editor, and had to co-ordinate all the production work with the German filmmakers and printers. James' German in the early days was, to say the least, limited. It always brought howls of laughter around the office when he would be heard screaming down the phone something like:

"Nein! Nein! Wir must haben the proofs zuruck by vier o'clock today. Nicht tomorrow!"

James interviewed so many top show business, rock and sports stars - usually when they were touring and performing in Germany. The Rolling Stones, Diana Ross, Santana, Freddy Mercury, John McEnroe and so many more all received the James Kitfield treatment. Incidentally, he worshiped the Stones so much he went to four of their concerts on consecutive nights just to watch their performance! Jumping ahead a few years, James was to become a very fine writer and journalist. He won the Gerald Ford Award for defence journalism on two occasions and received a cheque for $5000 each time. His 1995 book 'PRODIGAL SOLDIERS' is regarded as one of the finest accounts of the changing face of the U.S. military from the Vietnam period right through to the Gulf War. He currently lives and works for a defence trade journal in Washington DC working the Pentagon and mixing with top military brass and political leaders. He was embedded with the V Corps during the invasion on Iraq in March 2003 and tells some horrendous stories including how an incoming Iraqi missile killed one of his fellow journalists on the road to Baghdad.

LIVING WITH GERMANS (1976)

For our family, domestically, things went quite well - for a while that was. I spent those early weekends and evenings house hunting in Germany. I would telephone home to England everyday, check that Martin had done his homework and find out how Andy got on in her exams. Colin would tell me the news from school and I would tell them about Germany and the progress I was making in finding us a home. I flew back once for the weekend but it took me just six weeks to find us an attractive house to rent in a small town on the north side of the Taunus hills called Braunfels. We shipped some of our furniture from Brighton to Braunfels, leaving enough in the house in Brighton so we could rent it furnished.

I had missed the kids like crazy and it would have been so nice if we could have all stayed together but it was definitely better for Martin to remain in England for the first year. I drove to England to pick up the family including our beautiful Shetland sheepdog, Tricia. We had an uneventful ferry crossing and the 300-mile drive from Calais through Belgium to Braunfels. We arrived at just about the same time as the removal van and had so much fun unpacking and sorting everything out. Big decisions had to be made in deciding which bedroom each of us would have and then arranging and rearranging everything. Even Sigi seemed to enjoy herself. Progress, I thought.

The house was quite large, built on four levels on the side of hill. The summer of '76 was one of the hottest on record with almost perpetual sunshine making the views from our new home over the beautiful surrounding countryside even more stunning.

Third born Colin in Belgium on the way to our new life in Germany. Summer 1976

We had agreed that Andy and Colin would go to German schools and both quickly adapted to their new environment. On the day we moved in, Colin had made friends with a local kid and his German improved rapidly. By the time he went to school on the first day of the new term, he understood the basics. Within a few months, he was as good as the natives. At the age of six, it was easy. Likewise Andy. At the age of 14, she soaked it up like a sponge. My German was good enough to order meals in restaurants, be polite to the neighbours and to make some sense of the news and variety shows, but is was not good enough to follow the political and other serious discussions on TV - which were things which I really wanted to watch and listen. Sigi would sometimes translate for me but she soon got bored with that.

It was a twenty-minute car ride from Braunfels to the office in Friedrichsdorf through the beautiful Taunus hills. A days work and a home arrival time of around 6.30pm (late by German standards who tend to start early and finish early) gave me a couple of hours with Andy and Colin before spending the rest of the evening, reading 'Stars & Stripes' newspaper in 20 minutes flat, sitting in front of the TV with a drink trying to make some head or tail of what was going on. We all missed good old British telly - even Sigi admitted to that one. BBC Radio 2 was on the Long Wave in those days, which we could get reasonably clear in Braunfels. Colin and I would stay in bed late on Saturday mornings listening to Ed 'Stewpot' Stewart on 'Children's Choice' and fall about in fits of laughter every time we heard the famous "'ello darlin'!" Once the football season started, we were glued to the radio at 5 o'clock (British Time) on a Saturday to hear if the Seagulls had won. I really missed watching the games.

But Germany was OK - the job was good, Andy and Colin had settled down, Martin was working well at school and seemed to be getting on fine with his ersatz parents. Sigi soon became friendly with the neighbours and despite her parents being only an hour away, she still wasn't a happy lady.

Back at work, the magazine started to do really well. The new image was working. I was covering many autobahn kilometres visiting both regular and potentially new advertisers and making presentations and selling pages. The advertisers were located all over Germany plus Switzerland, Holland, Belgium and England. Sometimes I would fly, but mostly drove. And I would certainly make the most of the sales trips to England - getting together with Martin, going to the Goldstone ground to watch the Seagulls, then stocking up with Marmite and British comics for Andy and Colin before driving back to Germany.

Within a couple of months, work was about to take another dramatic turn. European advertising sales were picking up fine. But in the U.S.A. and Japan business was flat. Judd had appointed a media rep company in New York to sell ads in *'Overseas Life'*. The outfit was PABCO who themselves published one of the other military magazines, *'Family'*. In return, we at *'Overseas Life'* had been appointed to sell ads in Europe for *'Family'* magazine. The arrangement just wasn't working - primarily because we were far more interested in our own babies than someone else's.

In Japan, our reps were Media Sales Japan Inc. They were a good medium sized media rep company whose biggest title was the *'International Herald Tribune'*. Judd had visited Japan only on one occasion (to talk to MSJ) but never had any client or agency meetings. All communication was by phone, mail and telex. We did some business with Sony, Kenwood, Asahi Pentax etc in Japan but, naturally, most of MSJ sales efforts were directed towards the *'IHT'* where the big bucks were.

TOMORROW, THE WORLD! (1977)

One Monday morning I arrived in the office and just settled down at my desk with my first cup of coffee of the day, when Judd burst in very theatrically and asked me if I would like to take over worldwide advertising sales. I was gobsmacked. Yesterday - England, today - Europe and tomorrow - literally the world. Naturally, I asked him what he had in mind regarding pay etc. He threw a few figures at me and him not being a salesman, shocked me when he tried to close the deal on the spot. I asked for time to consider his proposal and told him I had seven appointments lined up in Frankfurt during the day and that I would be in the office same time tomorrow to give him my answer. I made my sales visits as quickly as possible and got home early. Out came the spreadsheet and calculator and I really burnt the midnight oil that night.

The money I had been earning in Germany so far had been good but, due to the fact I was an employee of Overseas Life Verlags GmbH, I had to pay full German taxes including the dreaded kirchensteur - church tax. If there was only a way of avoiding these taxes...and there was. At that time, under British tax rules, if you were employed by a British company but spent more than 300 days out of the country each year, you would get a 100% tax break. So why not form my own British company and become an employee of my own company? Then my company would negotiate a contract with Overseas Life Verlags GmbH to sell advertising globally on a commission only basis.

I obviously knew what the current total net advertising revenues from Europe were at the time and had approximate figures for U.S.A and Japan. I made projections, did some calculating and came up with figures that showed me how much I could potentially make. Things looked good - really good.

Next morning, Judd was already in when I arrived. I strutted into his office and boldly announced, "I'm resigning!". Poor Judd. I shouldn't have done it. I thought he was going to pass out as his face drained of colour. But I quickly revived him with, "But how about this for a proposition, Judd?" I explained my plan - I wanted just a straight 7.5% of all advertising revenues.

"No basic salary?"

Nope.

"No company car?"

Nope.

"No expenses?"

Nope.

We shook on the deal and at last I had the potential to earn a lot of money - all tax-free - legally.

Another quick trip back to England with two objectives in mind - to watch the Seagulls again and to form a company. I was a happy man. Brighton won the match and the company was formed with the help of Geoff Davis, my new accountant. I returned to Germany and immediately went to the local town hall and deregistered my residence - although continuing to spend most of the time there. A situation that was illegal under German law, but a chance worth taking. If I had continued as an official resident in Germany, I would still be liable to German taxes on my worldwide income.

With me now having to pay attention to the States and Japan, 'Overseas Life' needed a salesman for Europe. We took on Tom Harrington, an ex army captain who had piloted helicopters in Vietnam. He had married a German lady while stationed at Rhein-Main Air Base and now lived in a town not too far from the office. Tom had no real sales experience but was full of good personal qualities and I felt he would train easily and I could get him up and running quite quickly. I was right. He was soon earning me substantial override commissions. He took over my old company car and I bought myself a nifty Datsun 180B SSS coupe from a dealer in Brighton. Now it was off round the world - not in the Datsun but Pan Am First Class - in order to get the Americans and Japanese to start earning me even more money.

MADISON AVENUE STYLE

I telexed the guys at PABCO in New York telling them I wanted to come to visit clients for a couple of weeks. They, reluctantly I feel, agreed. Around that time, the magazine had an excellent trade-out or barter agreement with Pan

American Airlines with which we swapped advertising space for airline tickets. Judd had agreed that I could use the tickets freely as the agreements ran for one year at a time and we would lose the airline tickets if they weren't used by December 31. So, of course, almost all the travel was on Pan Am.

I booked flights from Frankfurt to New York via London, of course, on a Saturday morning to give me enough time to get to the Goldstone by three o'clock kick-off time. I stayed the night in Brighton, before travelling on to New York on the Sunday. I was in the PABCO office on Lexington Avenue early on Monday morning and met the boss man - Joe Mugnai - who greeted me with

New York, New York. A very happy hunting ground for me and a million other pro salesmen - but certainly not for the timid. It's so sad that the twin towers of the World Trade Center won't be seen again.

typical New York friendliness. His first lieutenant, Joe Araneo, also sat in on the meeting. Although on the surface everything was cordial, underneath I knew they were saying, "Who the hell does this Brit think he is? He comes here to Madison Avenue thinking he's going to teach us how to sell advertising?!" They gave me every reason why it was just about impossible to sell pages in 'Overseas Life' in the U.S. and suggested we spend the time with them teaching me how to sell pages for 'Family' magazine in Europe. My response was short and direct to the point -

"Like hell! On my nickel, we do things my way! If you want to teach me how to sell pages in 'Family', you can get your arses (or should I say 'asses') to Frankfurt any time you like and I will give you all the time in the world. Meanwhile, I am going to pitch you on the new 'Overseas Life', and then you can set up appointments over the next two weeks with the following key accounts and their agency people - Phillip Morris, Seagram, General Motors, Bose Corporation, Audiovox, JBL, Infinity," and the list went on.

They were frozen to their chairs, eyes and mouths wide open. I had earned their immediate respect and we all became great friends. That is the way it is with most Americans - you have to be big and bold and come on strong. We did the rounds on Madison Avenue, travelled up to Boston and down to New Jersey, west to Chicago, Louisville and on to the coast. I sold a lot of pages in the process and felt reluctant to pay PABCO their commission when I had done most of the work! I regularly visited the U.S. from then on always selling many pages on my trips. But PABCO didn't seem to sell many in between my visits and that was a lesson I learnt. Don't rely on a freelance media rep company or any other form of sales agent to do the business for you. Try to train and motivate them but if that doesn't work, then get out there and do it yourself.

VIVA LAS VEGAS!

In early January every year, Las Vegas hosts the huge winter Consumer Electronics Show (CES). And until it was dropped several years ago, the summer CES was held in Chicago in early June. Both shows lasted four days and you could hit all the major hi-fi and electronics customers in that time. Those shows were a very cost and time effective method of selling and became regular dates on my calendar. Las Vegas is a wonderful but probably the craziest place in the world. I don't think there is any other place that is so blatantly focused on dragging those dollars out of your wallet. Four days and nights is enough for me in Vegas but I have had some great times there. I would ask a few important clients to join me for dinner, a show and maybe a little gambling and some great times were had by all. Frank Sinatra live at the Sands, Shirley McClain in her one-woman show, Cirque de Soleil and the list could go on.

Overall, selling in the States is a dream. Unlike the U.K. where, for many, selling has been a dirty word and all sorts of defensive barriers spring up any time there is a salesman around, things are totally different over there. In the U.S. people like and expect to be sold to. If, at a party, you ask an american what he or she does for a living, they say, "I'm a salesman. I sell burger buns." And they say it with pride. Ask the same question at a party in England and you get all sorts of evasive answers like 'consultant', 'adviser', 'broker', 'account manager' or "I'm in PR" - when they are not in PR at all but are actually on the road selling double-glazing or baby foods to supermarkets. Just what has been the problem? Have the lawyers and accountants done such a great PR job in convincing us mere mortals that they are the only true 'professionals'? And that the rest of us are pond life? I really don't understand it.

Breaking into Fort Knox is easier than trying to fix an appointment with some of the media buyers at a London advertising agency. Layers of protection in the form of secretaries and assistants to get through, make life so difficult. On Madison Avenue, a quick call along the lines - "Hi, my name is Derek Halling and I want to visit you to give you a 10 minute pitch on a new publication" or "I've got some fresh ideas and a proposition I want to put to you," - will almost always get you a positive response. You arrive at the prearranged time and you make your pitch. You will always get an immediate reaction from the buyer - "I like it. We should be able to include your book in some of our client's ad schedules" or "Forget it - no chance." And if you are turned down, you will always be given the real reasons - not excuses. That's my style. Cut the waffle, cut the bullshit - and know where you stand at all times.

Then came Japan. And that was a totally different story. The business we were already getting from Japan was OK but *'Off Duty'* magazine was wiping the floor with us. Walter Rios had spent many years nurturing the Japanese electronics and camera companies and his efforts had really paid off. Walter was really the 'father' of the overseas military markets. He spent several years simply making the manufacturers aware that the market existed and the extra huge potential it offered. He supplied statistical market information, attended all the trade association meetings all over the world and generally did a great job in promoting the market and consequently, his magazine. I got no satisfaction and felt somewhat sad when Walter and his wife Dagmar eventually declared bankruptcy in the late '90s owing many millions of dollars.

DOING IT THE JAPANESE WAY

But back in the '70s, The *'Off Duty'* organisation was very substantial. They had offices in Frankfurt, New York, Los Angeles and Hong Kong with around 2 or 3 salesmen operating out of each office. They were getting 48, 72 or sometimes even 108 pages (at over US$10,000 per page) in a contract year from some the majors like Sony or Panasonic. This compared to our 12 or maybe 24 pages at less than $5,000 per page. Even the small A5 format family oriented books like Andy Anderson's *'R&R'* or Robert Beltz' *'AFN TV Guide'* were doing as well as we were.

I planned my first visit to Japan and started to make the airline reservations -

Pan Am, of course. Judd shocked me somewhat when he asked whether Sigi would like to go with me. He explained that we had more than enough in the pot and we would loose it if we didn't use it. Why not? I thought. Maybe it would cheer her up. The problem was that in the late seventies, Pan Am only flew to Tokyo from Frankfurt on the southern route. That meant one hell of a journey with stops in Teheran, Delhi, Bangkok and an overnight stay in Hong Kong before flying on to Tokyo the next day. All the glamour of first class lounges, first class welcome on board, first class champagne and first class multi-course meals on the upper deck of the Boeing 747 did cheer her up - but not for long. She was soon

Michinori (Michi) Okada was, and probably still is, one of the best Japanese salesmen selling advertising in Tokyo. He currently heads up his own media rep organisation - Tandem Inc.

complaining about airline food, long queues for immigration, indeterminate waits for baggage to arrive and so on and so on and so on. It was the same in the luxury Tokyo hotel where we were to stay for ten nights. The restaurant served an extensive range of Japanese and international fare but nevertheless she still managed to whinge about lack of choice and there being too many Japanese items on the menu! I was hoping that the message was at last sinking in with her that foreign travel was not always preferred to staying home and having peanut butter sandwiches with the kids. Her miserable attitude did preoccupy my thoughts when I should have been concentrating solely on the business side of things. After all, it was a business trip.

Tadashi Mori, one of the smallest Japanese gentlemen I was ever to meet, owned Media Sales Japan. His number two was Michinori Okada - one of the tallest! Morisan was no salesman but Michi, as he asked us to call him, was a terrific salesman. Some say he was too aggressive by Japanese standards. The Japanese style is very low key. The well-planned, well-documented approach is what is called for. Not the hit'em hard verbally style I had used a few weeks earlier in the States but the pleasantly, positive explanatory approach fully supported by information on paper is a must in Japan. Many American business people trying to sell something to the Japanese have failed miserably due to lack of understanding of the Japanese way. I was nothing if not flexible and handled the Japanese business with immediate good results. Over the next 23 years, I made over 50 trips to Japan during which time sales continued to grow and grow.

On that first visit, Michi had fixed a very busy schedule mainly in Tokyo but also in Hamamatsu where Yamaha was located and Osaka to see Minolta and a few others. We visited both manufacturers who were supplying the PXs and their ad agencies like Dentsu and Hakuhodo who, incidentally, happened to be the largest advertising agencies in the world during that era.

We travelled around by subway, bullet train, plane and taxis. Tokyo is always so crowded and busy. The air-conditioned, very clean taxis are very comfortable but often the drivers do not always know where they are going. So much for Japanese efficiency, I thought. Compared to London cabbies that had the 'knowledge', Tokyo was a nightmare. The streets were so crowded that you often remained still in the taxi for ages and feared being late for the next appointment. And punctuality is an important part of the Japanese culture. The subway is usually the quickest and most reliable way of getting around but the next train always seems packed as it arrives at the platform. Somehow we squeezed aboard travelling 15 stops packed like proverbial sardines. On arrival at our destination, Michi would stride ahead through the crowd with me trailing 15 or 20 yards behind. Luckily, he was so tall that I could see him through the masses of little people! Days like that were exhausting but completely satisfying.

The meetings usually took the traditional format of us one side of the table and two or three, sometimes more from the client or agency side, on the other side of the table. Business cards were exchanged and green tea or coffee always offered and accepted. The large ashtray in the centre of the table, filled very quickly with half smoked cigarettes. I would usually start the more formal part of the meeting by introducing myself and my product or proposal (in English, of course) for around ten minutes. I would back up everything I said with leaflets and other support material. That made it so much easier for those Japanese who could understand written English better than spoken English. Having said that, I was often complimented by the Japanese on my perfect English diction that they could very clearly understand! And me, a south London boy!

After my pitch, Michi would repeat the whole thing in Japanese. I would pay very close attention, never allowing myself the opportunity to sit back and appear to lose interest. A few more polite questions from the senior client person present such as, "How long do you stay in Japan?" and that was it. Shake hands all round and the meeting was over. Much bowing took place as we left the building before making our way back to the subway station. Unlike in the States, you almost never got any feedback at the meeting. They would go away and disperse copies of the information you had given them to all interested parties up and down their organisation - including their military rep companies. Consensus was their way. No one would make decisions unless everyone agreed - and that took time.

The next thing we would hear was the telex bursting into life back in the office in Germany a few weeks later. Out the paper would pour and it would read something like -

Dear Derek
Pleased to confirm 2 page, 4 Color spread for Pioneer every issue Jan thru Dec at $9800 gross per insertion. Films and official order to follow from K&L Best regards, Michi.

I would whoop with delight. The Germans in the office would be wondering what the crazy Brit was up to this time. Judd would say, "who's a clever boy then?" and the whole process would hopefully take place again the next day when the telex would inform us that, as a result of our meeting in Tokyo, Sony was increasing its order to 36 pages. That was magic. And then Tom Harrington would phone in to say he has just closed a deal to get BMW in the book for the first time. And that was even more magic.

THE LUSH LIFE OF ARIZONA

Change, once again, was lurking just around the corner. Judd's friend Stanley did not like Germany. He wasn't doing too many gigs. The Frankfurt Opera contract had expired and basically, he sat around at home all day devising ways of spending the money that Judd was making with the magazine. He was a wine connoisseur who would search for rare vintages and pay outrageous amounts of money for them. This would infuriate Judd and, like me with Sigi, he did not seem to be able to control these wild excesses of behaviour. Stanley was bored and wanted to go back to the States. He talked Judd into opening an office in Scottsdale, Arizona. We all panicked but unnecessarily so. Judd decided to keep the office in Germany and also open a new office in the States. He justified his position by saying how well the revenues and profits had grown over the past year or so and what was good enough for Walter Rios, was good enough for him! After opening the new office he left the rest of us in Germany to take care of our responsibilities in our own way. It sort of worked - but led to a good deal of pettiness around the office without having one person in charge.

Naturally, I had to visit Judd for business discussions and I just loved his new location. The new office was actually in Fountain Hills - a growing community in the Arizonan desert about 15 miles from Phoenix or Scottsdale. Saguaro cactus everywhere - totally beautiful with fantastic mountain views and sunsets.

Fountain Hills, as a small town, represented so much what appealed to me about the American enterprise culture. Development had been slow with property sales weak for quite a few years. Enter a marketing man with the idea that something exceptional needed to be done to get things really moving. The answer? A man-made lake with the highest fountain in the world! Higher even than Geneva. The fountain shoots high into the air every hour on the hour for ten minutes. The attraction proved irresistible and the tourists poured in. So many liked what they saw they stayed. Instead of buying a house or apartment in Scottsdale or Phoenix, they bought in Fountain Hills. Again, I'm glad the moneymen did not call the shots on that one. They would have asked all sorts of stupid questions and the fountain would never have been built. Fountain Hills would never have prospered to become the wonderful community it is today.

My 1981 office base in Fountain Hills, near Phoenix, Arizona. A great experience but doomed to failure due to non-cooperative spouses.

Arizonan summers were like hot - up to 115 degrees or more but with virtually no humidity. Winters, 70 something - nice. A great place, I thought. Judd and Stanley had bought a beautiful house, with a pool naturally, not too far from the office and they always invited us to stay to avoid unnecessary hotel bills. Their hospitality was generous and the evenings always kicked off with cocktails. Stanley would have his extra dry Tanqueray martini and Judd his Tanqueray straight up with a green olive - every evening. This was their ritual. James, myself or whoever else was in town, could choose from their extensive bar. One drink was fine, then the 'divi' - a new expression for me. Apparently it was short for 'dividend' - a smaller portion of your first drink and then no more! Apart from wine with dinner, that was it. Anything more than two drinks, meant, according to Stanley, you were a 'lush' and had some sort of problem! After dinner drinks? Forget it! Us lads had to sneak the bottle of Remy Martin outside around the pool after Stanley had gone to bed. Sometimes Judd would join us to put the world to right over a nightcap - but he was terrified Stanley would find out!

They had only been living there for a few months when Stanley was complaining again. This was wrong, that was wrong - maybe they should consider buying a home in Paradise Valley. Paradise Valley was, of course, an even more expensive up-market location. Those guys were making the self same mistake that those in Cranleigh had made ten years earlier - biting off more than they could chew. But I did not realize it fully at the time.

Meanwhile, Sigi had been stamping her foot quite vehemently recently, saying that she would never live anywhere other than Germany and certainly not England. What bothered me were the kids. Martin had spent his one-year alone in England followed by a year in Germany. He made a complete hash of his time in Germany. He couldn't efficiently cope in the new language. We discussed what was best for his future and he said he would like to go back to England to get his GCE 'A' levels. One more request from Martin - would it be OK for him to live alone in our own house? At the age of 17, that was some request! It meant no rental income for us, but who cared? I was making a lot more money and the responsibility would help

My Chevy parked outside our home in Scottsdale, Arizona sporting the Seagulls sticker. Catching the English football results meant having to have your ear glued to a Sony short wave radio at about 9 am on a Saturday morning. Strange!

Martin grow up quickly. And that's what I wanted more than anything else in the world - for my kids to grow up to be responsible adults and stand on their own two feet. Martin responded magnificently. Apart from a few noisy parties (reported to me later by vigilante neighbours) and a few teenage tricks like hoisting some underwear up a local councillor's flagpole, nothing untoward happened. What's more, I could sleep in our own house when I was in England. But I always played fair with Martin and phoned to say I was on my way home and give him a chance to get the place relatively straight.

Andy and Colin were a different story...they were becoming very German. Nothing against the Germans of course, but I really didn't like the idea of my kids growing up to become German. International fine, but German no. By this time, Andy had a German boyfriend - quite a decent guy on the surface but he had been arrested a couple of times for not too serious offences. Just a part of growing up, I thought - she will find Mr. Right later and hopefully not in Germany. And she did.

Then along came another big opportunity. On one of my regular visits to Arizona, Judd threw this one at me:

"European and Japanese sales are growing nicely, but American sales could do with some more help. How about you living over here? We could fire PABCO and directly employ one or two sales guys. That should really help things along." Quite frankly, for the work I was doing, I could be based just about anywhere - even back in England. But there was no way that Sigi would agree to that one. But she may just go along with living in Arizona. We called her in Braunfels from Judd's office and painted a rosy picture of life in the Valley of the Sun. You know the sort of thing - cocktails around the pool, the bright lights of Las Vegas and Hollywood not being too far away, and so on. She bought it. Andy had left regular school in Braunfels and was attending a full-time, live-in college in Limburg studying kindergarten teaching. Martin was happy with his studies and his life in Brighton. So it was Sigi, Colin and myself who packed our bags for a new life in the sun. That was an opportunity I had been waiting for - the full time link with Germany had been broken.

There were a few minor problems like U.S. immigration authorities to worry about. We told the officer at Kennedy airport that we were on an extended business trip lasting about six months - the longest they would give you for permission to stay at any one time. But what about the boy? I mumbled something about private tutors and, lo and behold, he stamped our passports and we were through. We had intended to pay for Colin to go to private school but right opposite the house we rented in East Hearn Road in Scottsdale was a regular American school called 'Sandpiper'. I arranged a meeting with the headmaster and asked if there was any chance of Colin being able to attend their school. "We would just love to have Colin attend our school," came the warm and friendly american-style response. I must admit, I did feel a little guilty about

Colin being educated at the american tax payers expense - oh, what the hell...

So it was a two-minute walk to school for Colin and a twenty-minute drive to the office for me through the beautiful Arizonan desert to Fountain Hills.

Judd provided a decent office for free and agreed to pay all my phone calls. I would have to pay for everything else like the house rental, car rental, airplane tickets and so on. Also, I still had fairly sizable outgoings in the form of allowances for Martin and Andy plus her college fees.

A tiny alarm bell started ringing when Judd told me they had sold the house in Fountain Hills and bought a far larger place in Paradise Valley. Some place, I thought, on my first visit - almost Beverly Hills style.

Within a few weeks of arriving in Arizona I flew back to Europe - saw Martin in Brighton (with a visit to the Goldstone of course - we won 3-0) and Andy in Germany. Checked that the office in Friedrichsdorf was still there and that Tom Harrington was still doing the business and afterwards reported back to Judd. A routine visit to Japan and then we started interviewing for two guys as salesmen for the U.S. Judd and myself flew to New York, terminated the agreement with PABCO and employed a very experienced space salesman called Dan O'Leary to cover the east coast and the mid west based near La Guardia airport.

Interviewing a short list of names at a recruitment consultant's office in old town, Scottsdale, one stood head and shoulders above all the others - a guy called Tom Bowers. Like the other Tom in Germany, he had had little experience but was an outstanding, personable young man of 23. Tom became a great salesman and a close personal friend. Tom Bowers had just settled down covering all the business on the coast and the south west, when Tom Harrington called from Germany to say he had been offered a job with a big Frankfurt advertising agency that came with a massive pay rise and would therefore have to resign. We couldn't stand in his way, so he went. Tom Bowers was in the Fountain Hills office when the call came through and wasted no time in asking if we would

consider him for a move to Europe. Why not? And within weeks, Tom had settled down in the Friedrichsdorf office and selling pages like they were going out of style. James Kitfield and Tom Bowers became good friends too and soon were sharing an apartment in a small town called Morfelden, just south of the Frankfurt airport. Little did I realise

Fun times in Arizona in 1981. From left to right: Colin, myself, Andy and her friend Kiki.

at the time that James and Tom were, in the not too distant future, to become my landlords!

Everything was going just fine - the magazine was looking good and we were selling ever-increasing amounts of advertising pages. I would submit an invoice to Judd monthly for my override commissions and he would cut me a cheque.

One particular month, as I gave Judd my invoice, he looked a little awkward:

"Er, Derek, I don't know how to say this, but...but...we are having cash flow problems at the moment and I won't be able to pay you the full amount this month.

"Say, what?!" came my hesitant reply, "How can this be? Business has never been better! All our customers are paying on time - just what is the problem?"

"Well, what with the additional expense of this and that, things are just tight right now. I promise you I'll make it up next month."

Well, he didn't make it up next month either. More excuses - but no more money. He should have paid me say $12,000 commission for the month, but would only pay me $6000. This went on for a few months before I fully realised what had been going on. The cost of their new home was very high - even by American luxury standards. Stanley's taste in wall coverings and drapes was in keeping with his taste in fine wines. They ate in only the best restaurants in town and all this was being sucked out of Judd's business - at my expense!

At around the same time, Martin, Andy and a friend of hers, Kiki, came to visit for a vacation. It was great fun. We were all together having a lot of laughs but underneath it all, I was feeling very insecure. We did the Grand Canyon, Disneyland and all the other good things that tourists do and the kids were due to fly back within a few days. I gave Judd an ultimatum that unless he paid me what he owes me; I was leaving with the kids on that plane back to Europe. If he could not pay in full, there and then, I would accept a part payment programme that would substantially cut the overdue amounts. In that case, I would continue to do what I had been doing but based out of our fully paid-for home in England.

No lump sum was forthcoming, so it was back to England. The whole family stopped off at the New York Hilton for a couple of days of more tourist activity and it was home to Brighton, just in time to watch Charles and Diana get married in the Summer of '81.

Of course, Sigi had done her usual song and dance routine about not wanting this or not wanting that, but by this time, I had just about finally had enough of her. I placed Sigi and Stanley in the same category of partners - those that always seem to manage to screw up so many good things.

No further payments were received from Judd. I obviously could not continue on that basis and was effectively out of work.

Judd French finally owed me just over $25,000, which, in itself at that time, was quite substantial, but not enough to get all screwed up about. I took the attitude that I had earned so much more over the past five years compared to what I would have earned at Remington and Judd had helped to make this possible. There was no way I was going to shoot him in the kneecaps or anything. Of course, I tried to get paid, but when I found out he owed the printers in Ireland money, plus quite a few others too, I wrote it off to experience.

TIME OUT IN ENGLAND (1981-1982)

I took time out and enjoyed England. It was great getting Colin settled back into his old school and him meeting all his English friends once again. Martin was pleased to have his younger brother around full time, while Andy had one more year to finish at college in Germany but came home at every opportunity she could.

I was beginning to worry about money, and as my dad had told me all those years earlier - "keep the money coming in" - and I had to do just that.

Two guys, a German based in Frankfurt and an American in New York, already in the publishing side of the military market, had decided to start a new military sports magazine. They asked me to sell some ads for them, and I agreed. I did one trip to the States and a couple to Germany for them and sold quite a few pages for the first edition. On one of the trips to Germany, after driving Sigi to see her parents in Neustadt an der Wied, I had gone on alone to Berlin and Frankfurt. On returning to my in-laws, Sigi informed me she would stay on for a few days and would make her own way back to England by train. I returned home where we all waited for her. She never phoned us and when we phoned her, she made some excuse that she would have to stay a little longer.

On the last trip to Germany, I found out that the sports magazine people were printing thousands and thousands fewer copies than they told me and the advertisers they were printing. Little did they know that I had good friends at the printers who kept me well informed. I challenged them - but, of course, they denied everything. I obviously could not continue being associated with liars and cheats. A prompt resignation followed. I had been selling for over twenty years and had never, ever sold anything to anyone based on a lie. Professional salesmen sometimes bend or evade the truth ever so slightly, but never, ever, blatantly lie.

Four months later, Sigi was still not back. I phoned yet again and spoke to mother-in-law who informed me that Sigi had rented a flat back in Braunfels! That was it, I thought, and then had to make full time arrangements to have my eleven-year-old Colin taken care of while I went out to work. I employed a live in 'nanny'. I would get him off to school every morning and she would be there when he came home. Martin would come back from college a little later and I would arrive home around seven. It worked quite well.

I did some marketing consultancy work for a souvenir spoon company based in Brighton and, at the same time, a new non-military London based magazine called *'Worldwatch'*. I was generally advising them of the best methods of maximising their advertising and other non-subscription revenues. It all paid the bills but was not too exciting or rewarding.

In the autumn of 1981, Judd managed to sell the magazine for just $100,000 - but all the creditors were swooping. Judd didn't get a penny. The new owners were a partnership comprising of Mr E 'Andy' Anderson, owner of *'R&R'* magazine based in Heidelberg, Germany and Mr Murry Greenwald, owner of EBM Inc which, in turn owned *'Exchange and Commissary News'*, a military trade publication out of Westbury, New York.

Andy Anderson was a super nice guy who I knew quite well. He was to run *'Overseas'* magazine (the title it had become since the *'LIFE'* magazine forced us to drop 'life' from our title) in Germany and Murry Greenwald's team would be the U.S. advertising rep company. Andy Anderson closed down the office in Friedrichsdorf and opened up a more central office directly opposite the main station in Frankfurt. James Kitfield was kept on as editor. Tom Bowers was still responsible for European sales and Vivienne Reeve was the new girl Friday.

Suddenly one day at home in Brighton, I heard a key go in the front door. Everyone was in, so I thought who the hell could this be? Right, Sigi. Out of the blue, as bold as brass, she stood there and announced that she was home - for good. Could I trust her? I shouldn't have done but I had to take the chance.

The reason I had to take this chance was that Andy Anderson, the new part owner of *'Overseas'* magazine, had telephoned asking if I was interested in having my old position back. I told him then and there that there was no way that I would live full time in Germany. He invited me to Heidelberg for a chat and explained a few things to me. Advertising sales were not good, and they needed a big hitter - like Derek Halling - in the team. If I wasn't interested in living permanently in Germany, what about commuting each week? Monday to Friday in Frankfurt then weekends in Brighton? At least that way I could watch the Seagulls play on a Saturday afternoon. I couldn't afford the money for the flights each week I told him. "Don't worry about that," he replied, "We have exchange agreements in place with World Airways and British Caledonian who both fly Gatwick/Frankfurt everyday, and so the flights won't cost you anything. You can use them plus TWA and American Airlines to pay for your trips to States and Japan too. I will provide a car for getting around while you are in Germany, but you will have to pay for your own accommodation during the week." Now the big question - money. We negotiated and struck a deal. But the success or otherwise of the situation once again revolved around my totally unreliable spouse.

COMMUTING FROM BRIGHTON TO FRANKFURT (1982-1984)

The next two years were very bittersweet. I would have great weekends with the kids watching the Seagulls and going to the movies and then back up to

The 1982 'Overseas' magazine team of (right to left) Andy Anderson, Tom Bowers and myself at a trade association meeting in Heidelberg, Germany in 1982.

Gatwick again on Monday for the early morning flight to Frankfurt. Ten minutes on the U-Bahn from the Flughafen to the Hauptbahnhof and two minutes later I was in the office - just over three hours door to door. I had a Mitsubishi Galant parked in the station underground car park and a season ticket supplied by Andy Anderson's firm. The small suite of offices in the Pan Am building housed about eight of us altogether. Tom Bowers and myself shared an office with three or four 'R&R' ad sales people in the next room. James Kitfield had his den and Vivienne Reeve had hers. Vivienne was another Brit who, with her husband John, had left the UK to settle in Germany in the late '70s. She was, and still is, an absolute darling - a real mother hen who kept all us crazy salesmen under some sort of control. With the big boss and his staff based an hour away in Heidelberg, she generally took care of all the office administration. Tom and myself sat side by side at desks with our backs to the window that overlooked the station. We often said that should a terrorist bomb go off in the station at anytime, flying glass would decapitate us! Six months later a bomb did go off in the nearby Iran Air office but it was relatively small and luckily, we were not in the office at the time.

The 'R&R' sales team of Johannes 'Fifi' Hengstenberg, Terri Violano, Helen Ball and John Wells with occasional visits from Williams (never did find out his first name), a trained-to-kill ex marine responsible for 'R&R' distribution, made the next office a fun place, too. They were all out of the 'work hard - play hard' mould. John Wells was a great salesman when he was sober but played too hard by binge drinking. He died falling out of his own bed onto a glass, which broke and severed a main artery. He did not know it even happened. He simply laid there bleeding to death - later to be found by his girlfriend in one huge pool of blood. Apart from that tragedy, it was a fun-like but very professional atmosphere. Things got done and we did a lot of business.

Tom Bowers and James Kitfield's apartment was about a twenty-minute drive from the office. It was quite spacious with a large living room, kitchen, bathroom and a separate bedroom for both. In the living room there was a huge settee that at one time had belonged to Judd and Stanley. That settee became my bed four nights most weeks for the next couple of years. I was 47 at the time and Tom and James were both 25 - but we all got on like a house on fire. They seemed more than happy to have me around and I certainly enjoyed their company. My weekly rent was a litre bottle of duty free Remy Martin that had to be paid promptly on arrival on a Monday morning but wouldn't get opened till Monday evening. That became the ritual. When we ate out, I would also pick up most of the tabs at the local Italian restaurant. But that one wasn't written into the rental agreement - the Remy was.

Being young healthy bachelors, James and Tom were always chasing the chicks. Despite Tom's dark good looks, he always managed to get the ugly or moody ones. James always got the crackers but occasionally he failed to score - even when it was on the proverbial plate. One lovely summer day, James called the office from Hamburg. He had been on a PR jolly with the Deutsche Bundesbahn (German Railways) and was due to arrive back at Frankfurt Station at seven that evening. Could we pick him up and give him a ride back to the flat? Tom and myself left the office around six-thirty and had just one pils in one of the local bars before wandering into the station to meet the seven o'clock arrival from Hamburg. James came back with more baggage than he went with - he had the most gorgeous young lady on his arm. She was German and beautifully groomed - a woman of class. Introductions all around and back to the flat. After a few drinks in the evening sunshine on the balcony followed by something to eat, it wasn't long before James and this gorgeous thing were nibbling at each others ears. Tom and myself smiled knowingly as the two of them slinked away in the direction of James' bedroom. Literally thirty seconds later she was gone! Another minute or so went by before James sulkingly came out of his room. "How could I have blown that one?" he vaguely questioned. Tom and myself didn't reply but casually strolled into his bedroom to find it in total chaos! An unmade bed with crumpled sheets not even covering the mattress, dirty underwear, smelly trainers, used towels, old copies of Penthouse and empty beer cans strewn everywhere. Really James - poor preparation had spoiled the close to that particular presentation!

Tom on the other hand was always immaculate. He dressed well, kept his room tidy and always made it back to his own bed at some stage of the night, irrespective of how many drinks he had had - and always bright eyed and bushy tailed ready for work at nine o'clock the next day. Except one particular morning:

The previous evening, Tom, James, Williams and myself had been out for a

Tom Bowers (standing), the nicest guy and probably the finest professional salesman encountered in my life, chats to Roy Hancock from Panasonic - one of the biggest buyers of advertising in the U.S. military market.

meal at the 'Alte Aenchen', a nice restaurant in the Sachenshausen district of Frankfurt. Tom had got an income tax rebate so we were celebrating with a meal and a couple of beers. We shared a cab back to the main station to pick up our cars. James and I had had enough. "Come on guys, just one more beer," Tom and Williams pleaded. James and I last saw them semi staggering across the street into Kaiser Strasse, the seedier part of Frankfurt, before we drove home for the usual Remy before going to bed.

When I was staying at their apartment, it was the morning ritual that Tom would use the bathroom first, me second and James last. This particular morning I glanced at my watch but could not hear Tom in the bathroom. It was later than usual. I jumped off the settee and noticed Tom's bedroom door was wide open with no Tom inside. Panic! James panicked too - Tom always made it home. We hurriedly dressed and were about to leave when the phone rang. "Hi guys..." - it was Tom. "Where the f*** are you?" I meekly inquired. "Don't worry. I'll see you in the office and tell you the whole story then. Bye."

The story went something like this:

Instead of choosing a regular bar or even a brothel for their 'just one more beer', the pair stupidly stumbled into a clip joint. You know, the sort of place where a girlie hostess drinks coloured water at 50 marks a glass. If she touches your knee, it's another 200 marks on the bill. When they came to leave, the bill was for over 2000 marks! They both almost passed out with the shock! On objecting, they were soon surrounded by some of the toughest looking Yugoslav mafia around, against who even ex-marine Williams didn't fancy his chances. With a collection of cash, credit cards and eurochecks, they managed to get out of the place. The bill came to more than Tom's tax rebate. Williams decided that Tom was too drunk to drive home and said he could stay at his place for the night. Williams' wife was a serving nurse major in American military, making Williams one of the few male spouses. The couple lived on an American military housing area in northwest Frankfurt about ten minutes drive away. At around 3 am, they had driven into the housing area to be confronted by the American military police. "Have you been drinking?" they demanded to know. Williams owned up to a few beers earlier and as a result, the German Polizei were called due to the fact the American MPs did not have breathalysers on board. Williams was last seen by Tom, who was now standing at the side of the road, being taken away in a German police van. He was shouting something like, "427 - apartment 427!" Tom went staggering around the housing area looking for apartment 427. On finding it, he rang the doorbell then waited a while. This robe-clad six-foot lady major eventually opened the door. "Your husband said I could sleep with you tonight!" blurted out Tom.

I just don't know how Tom survived that one - but that was Tom's charm, I suppose. To finish the story, Williams was right on the limit. He didn't lose his driving licence but he was detained by the police so didn't make it home until late the next afternoon. After that little episode, I don't think his wife talked to him for weeks.

Back to business. Even though I was freelance, Andy Anderson had given me the title of Advertising Director of 'Overseas' magazine that meant I still had total responsibility for all advertising revenues for the magazine, as I did under Judd French. I continued the long trips to Japan and did sales calls with Michi.

The flying times to Tokyo were coming down to around 16 hours with a choice of flights via Anchorage, Alaska or Moscow, Russia. Those flights were still tiring though. Jet lag for a few days after arrival, made things worst. I had a simple philosophy - work when you have to, eat when you are hungry (as long as it didn't interfere with your appointments), and sleep whenever and wherever you could. It worked for me and I was never late for a meeting.

Around that time, the Korean electronics manufacturers were taking notice of the U.S. military market, and were jealous of their Japanese competitors huge volume sales in the PXs. That meant additional sales calls for me on the likes of Samsung, Goldstar and Daewoo in Seoul. Dealing with the Koreans wasn't that much different from dealing with the Japanese but they did seem a little less formal and somewhat more American in their style.

The situation in the States was unique and interesting for me. EBM were my sales reps for the USA, but Murry Greenwald, the owner of EBM, also owned 50% of 'Overseas' magazine making him half my boss! He had some good sales guys working for him like Joe Haik, Jim Ocello and Bill Cobb and we would all get on well with each other.

I would fly into New York for a sales meeting which I had called in their offices to give them all, including Murry, a bad time for not closing this or that deal or why had Bose cut back on the number of pages. After my performance, Murry would cut in and say, "Have you finished, Derek? Now it's my turn and, as half your boss, why the hell haven't you done this or that?" The teamwork was great. We would all get together at least once a year - and that included most of the European team - at the ALA (American Logistics Association) National Convention which was held annually in, say, Washington DC or San

Francisco. Murry would always book the penthouse or presidential suite for EBM and everybody who was anybody in the military market would come by to chat and have a drink. *'Exchange & Commissary News'* was the trade 'bible' which pulled everyone in and the rest of us would hover and pounce, in a very professional way of course, whenever we saw an opportunity to interest the visitor in the possibility of advertising in our particular book.

A VERY EXPENSIVE FOOTBALL MATCH (1983)

On the football front, Brighton & Hove Albion did well by climbing out of the fourth division and eventually getting promotion to Division 1 in 1979. By 1983, they were heading for the pinnacle of English football - the FA Cup Final at Wembley Stadium. A Jimmy Case screamer of a free kick plus a nice Michael Robinson goal against Sheffield Wednesday saw us win the semi-final at Highbury. And that was it! "We were on our way to Wembley and we would not be moved!" we sang after the game all the way back to Brighton. We really couldn't believe it, but it was true.

The next problem was getting tickets for the final, which was to be held on Saturday 21st May and even Sigi wanted to go to the big one - even though she never had shown a flicker of interest before - which meant I had to queue up for hours to get five tickets. It was a fantastic day out and a fantastic game. The opposition was Manchester United. They were and still are, the mightiest club in the land but on the day, we were just as big. Arriving at the stadium three hours before the kick-off, we watched our team arrive by specially chartered British Caledonian helicopter. Seeing that helicopter swoop around Wembley Stadium in its special blue and white livery was one of those majestic images that will stay with me forever.

These tickets were like gold dust, but with the Seagulls in the Wembley Cup Final it was a 'must-be-there-once-in-a lifetime' match. The match was a draw after extra time, so we had a replay on the following Thursday. That caused me all sorts of logistical problems of just getting to the match from Germany - but I made it - just!

The game started and we scored first. Fantastic! But United came back strongly and we were 2 - 1 down. Things looked better when Gary Stevens blasted an equaliser to take the game into extra time. With only minutes to go of the extra 30 minutes, Brighton's Michael Robinson passed to Gordon Smith who had only the United goalkeeper to beat. "And Smith must score!" roared the TV commentator. But he didn't. The goalkeeper easily handled his tame shot. The final whistle blew. 2 - 2. And that meant a replay on the coming Thursday evening. We had done well but not quite well enough. Poor Gordon Smith - you must feel sorry for him. Everywhere he goes, even these days over 20 years on, he is apparently still recognised as the striker who missed that sitter for Brighton in the 1983 Cup Final.

The next day saw me queuing yet again for tickets for the replay. The Club had announced overnight that they would be giving priority to fans who were buying season tickets for the following season. That meant I had to buy five season tickets too! It was getting a bit expensive. It got even more expensive after I realised that I was scheduled to attend a very important two-day convention at the Frankfurt Airport Sheraton Hotel all day Thursday and Friday. Something that business wise simply could not be missed. On the other hand, there was no way I was going to miss the game either!

It took another of my devious plans to work that one out which went like this:

I flew back to Frankfurt the next morning as usual on British Caledonian from Gatwick. I then booked a flight on Lufthansa from Frankfurt to Heathrow to arrive at about 5.30pm on the evening of the replay, Thursday. Kick-off time 7.45pm. I also booked a Heathrow airport hotel room for the same night. I arranged for Sigi and the kids to pick me up at Heathrow then drive us all to Wembley for the match.

I sneaked out of the convention exactly as the afternoon session finished literally running across the bridge from the hotel into the terminal building and straight to the gate. Good old German efficiency, I thought - Lufthansa was on time. Sigi did not let me down this time as she was waiting with the kids as arranged. After the game, she dropped me back at the hotel at Heathrow where I managed a few hours sleep before catching the 7.30 flight next morning back to Frankfurt. Spot on starting time, I walked into the convention room with none of my colleagues or clients being any the wiser where I had spent the previous evening. At exactly the same time on the Friday, it was back across the same bridge to the terminal to catch the British Caledonian flight back to Gatwick to be home for the weekend. That, for me, was certainly the most

Martin and Colin on the way to the Goldstone Ground, the home of Brighton & Hove Albion Football Club for almost 100 years until the money men did an asset stripping job in 1997. The dodgy deal left the Club without their own ground and having to groundshare with Gillingham over 70 miles away, but returned to play back in Brighton at the Withdean Stadium in 1999.

The West Stand of the Goldstone Ground - where branches of Currys and Toys-R-Us are now located.

expensive football match of all time. By the way, the second game score was Manchester United 4, Brighton 0.

The kids and I watched the recording of the first match over and over again that weekend. Even these days, from time to time, I still dig out that video trying to convince myself that if I watch it often enough, one day Smith will score. We don't watch the recording of the replay very often....

PART IV

TIME TO DO MY OWN THING (COMPLETELY) (1984)

By 1984, I had been involved in the military market for eight years, but was still thought by many to be the 'new kid on the block'. But in reality, as far as the publishing side was concerned, I knew just about everything there was to know. I had achieved my earlier objective of making money by open-ended commission schemes and, by careful tax planning, kept most of it in my pocket. But, just when things were building up nicely, Judd French had let me down. Could the same thing happen again with Andy Anderson and Murry Greenwald? I was 49 but Anderson was getting up there around 70. What would happen should he retire? Would the magazine continue? These and many other questions had been going through my mind for a while. Nearing 50 years and with my life's ambition of seeing the kids grow up into worthwhile adults almost achieved, was the time right to do my own thing - completely independent of corporate bosses or controlling principals?

Martin was 23 doing well as a salesman selling finance and leasing deals. He did so well that a few years later he saw an opportunity of starting his own brokerage firm. Daughter Andy was working for Mentzendorf, the UK importers of Bollinger Champagne. She started with them as a receptionist cum clerical assistant, but I really wasn't so surprised when she came home one evening to announce that she was to be given an opportunity of entering sales. Andy became the very first on-the-road female sales person to sell Bollinger Champagne in the UK. She certainly grabbed that opportunity and made a fantastic success of it. Colin was getting good results at college - despite a few run-ins with teachers that I had to sort out. He was to go on to get a good degree at university and start a great career in journalism. The time was now right for me to make the big move.

The military market had peaked. The US dollar/Japanese Yen ratio was causing a few profit problems and putting pressure on advertising budgets. With some distant rumblings about troop reductions overseas, the competition for advertising was as vicious as ever. The electronics manufacturers would tell me that they could not support all the general interest military magazines in market. "OK, OK," they would say, " '*Overseas*' magazine is aimed at the young single GI - but that's only part of the story. What we really need is even more specialisation." The best salesman is the salesman who can listen. I listened and took careful note. I kept all these thoughts about specialisation in my mind for several months before coming to some final conclusions. Meanwhile, daily life went on.

Sigi was still driving me crazy. We were living separate lives in separate rooms in our home. Divorce petitions were flying in both directions. There were court appearances over just about everything - money, custody of Colin, selling the house. I simply could not talk to her. She had to take everything to court. She was getting legal aid but it was costing me an arm and a leg in legal bills. In addition, everything became so petty - she wouldn't take phone messages for me and she even stole my mail. With all this activity going on in England demanding my attention, I was hardly spending any time in Germany. And that did not please Andy Anderson too much. We discussed our mutual futures and worked out a formula for my gradual termination over the following months.

Tom Bowers had left 'Overseas' to work for a multi-language electronics trade magazine called 'ACE International'. A personable young american called Bob Snyder published the book in London but Tom would be working in the Netherlands. Tom had earlier taken a weekend trip to Amsterdam and met a 'nice' young lady called Karin. He fell in love and wanted to be with her in Amsterdam - hence the move. She turned out to be yet another spouse who delighted in making life as difficult as possible for her partner.

James Kitfield had followed his regular girlfriend Marjory, who had been a teacher at an american military school in Darmstadt, back to the States to live in LA before breaking up with her and moving to DC.

Vivienne Reeve saw her opportunity with the British forces in Germany. She and husband John started publishing a magazine for the brits titled 'The Key'. In other words, the old team was breaking up. New faces were appearing at 'Overseas' like Tina Dean, Alix Paultre and Ted Taylor. All good people but it would never be the same again.

A WEDDING IN AMSTERDAM (1984)

Despite Tom Bowers's departure to Amsterdam, I remained in constant touch with him as the years went by. You just felt good in his presence or in chatting to him on the phone. He had announced the wedding date to Karin and we were all invited. I had got to know one of Tom's school buddies from Arizona, Vance Riggins, when he had earlier visited Tom in Frankfurt. I was to meet more of his old friends at the big wedding in Amsterdam. Dan Mahon flew in from Phoenix with Sanders and Roxy Achen together with the Bowers family comprising Mum Polly, slightly younger brother Tim and sisters Patti and Betsy. Tom's Dad died when Tom was a teenager. Tom had told me often how much he missed his Dad and I guess he would have loved him to be there with them on his big day. Polly was a very strong, special sort of lady who had done a fantastic job in bringing up four kids without having her loving man around.

I missed out on the stag night, but judging by the look on their faces the next day, I'm glad I did! I arrived in Amsterdam on the morning of the wedding, checked into the hotel where I was staying, then made my way to the town hall where the ceremony was to take place. It was the shortest I had ever witnessed. A few words in Dutch followed by the same in English, an exchange of rings and it was all over. The rest of the day and night was spent celebrating. And what a celebration it was - good people, good food, good drink and good music. I only hoped that things would work out for them. I don't really know why, but I had my doubts even on their wedding day.

'ACE International' was in trouble. Bob Snyder, who had quit, was the only guy around who could really made it work. He had gone back to the States to be the publisher of a computer magazine. Tom was uneasy about the future of ACE and when Bob called him to offer a job selling space for his new publication, Tom was tempted. To be based in Boston, he was offered a very attractive package. Having talked it over with Karin, his new wife, they agreed that Tom would take the job and go ahead to Boston. Karin would finish a course she was attending and then follow Tom over. To cut a longish story short, he went but she didn't. Following excuse after excuse, finally Tom gave her a deadline. The deadline passed and divorce ensued...another spouse who had loused things up, I thought.

I felt so sorry for Tom - he really deserved a good woman. After that year's Summer CES in Chicago, I went through Boston to visit him. By this time, the divorce was final and Tom was dating a young american lady who turned out to be yet another straight out of the top draw bitch. I would always give Tom a bad time about his women - in a nice sort of way, of course.

"What's wrong with you Bowers?" I would say. "You are good looking sort of guy, but you always get involved with the wrong women." It turned out it was always the same when Tom was at high school and college. Dan Mahon later told me that he could have had the pick of the pack but, for reason or reasons unknown, he didn't.

The following January, I was scheduled, as usual, to go to the Winter CES in Las Vegas. Tom was too. We arranged to spend the four days at the show and then travel to Phoenix together - Dan Mahon was getting married. He and his bride-to-be, Michelle, had even changed the wedding date because of Tom's CES commitments - both so wanted Tom to be there. When they heard I was in town, I too was invited.

Tom had another good friend who was the marketing manager of one of Scottsdale's large resort hotels. When he heard Tom and I were coming to town, he offered us one of his best suites for the stay - free! "There's always a buffet going on in the hotel somewhere," he told us on arrival, "Just help yourselves." I liked Tom a lot and his friends just as much! We had a great stay culminating in the wonderful wedding where I met even more of Tom's friends. Lasting memories include just how beautiful Michelle looked and seeing Bill Segal stomping across the car park doing his imitation of a one eared elephant!

Incidentally, Michelle is a lovely lady who has supported Dan for many years in his speciality foods wholesale business. And all this while having to hold down her own job in insurance plus having a family - Megan now a teenager and a real sweetie. Despite my cynicism, Michelle helped a great deal in restoring my faith in the fact that there are some supportive spouses around.

THE BIRTH OF 'AVP SPECIAL REPORT' (1985)

That word 'specialisation' kept going around and around in my head. It made me do some serious thinking. Then it came to me - why not publish a magazine specialising in home electronics and photography for US military consumers? The upside of the situation was that I could live full time again in England with a clear conscience and call all the shots myself. The downside was that there was no way that I wanted to afford editors salaries etc, so I would have to do just about everything myself. That suited me fine. And so 'Audio Video Photo Special Report' or 'AVP Special Report' was conceived.

I decided the basic format would be:
*High quality glossy American A4 format making it very long life
*The same amount of advertorial space free with every ad purchased
*Two issues each year - Fall/Winter in October and Spring/Summer in April with separate European and Pacific editions
*Free copies to the reader and ONLY distributed only in those military retail facilities selling home electronics and photo merchandise
*As low as sensible advertising rates

The pitch would be a salesman's dream. The real clincher was that I would be targeting the audience precisely by distributing the magazine only in specialised retail outlets. In other words, no wasted copies - hence advertising dollars - in commissaries or young wives clubs whose clientele had little or no interest in hi-fi or serious photography. With so many monthlies around, the decision to go for only two issues a year was a real winner. Just about every manufacturer felt he could at least afford an ad twice a year - unlike all the other magazines that were constantly pushing for twelve times a year. For the free page of editorial, I would ask the advertiser to let us have leaflets, spec sheets and photographs and we would do the rest. We would write up the article featuring some of their models or maybe a company profile and maybe include a head and shoulders shot of their key person - just to stroke the ego a little you know!

I launched 'AVP Special Report' at the January 1985 Winter CES Show in Las Vegas for publication in the following October. I pitched just about everyone involved in selling home electronics to the U.S. military stationed overseas - especially the american based clients. I made a decision that personal contact twice a year at the winter and summer CES shows, plus plenty of phone, fax and later e-mail work in between, would enable me to personally handle U.S. sales. In addition, at some time or another, I would visit every client in his or her own office.

Covering the U.S.A. myself meant that there was no real need to appoint a rep company over there. That saved me 15% commission - a lesson I learned back in 1976 when we were paying PABCO a commission on all orders from the U.S.A. when I was actually closing most deals myself on my trips to the States.

On to Japan to meet up with Takeshi Miyaji who had recently quit Pioneer Electronics to form his own consultancy and media rep company known as Courtland Incorporated. MSJ were still representing *'Overseas'* magazine, so I couldn't use them to sell pages in Japan for *'AVP Special Report'*. Tak and I agreed terms with no written contract or other fancy stuff cooked up by lawyers. A few key points of agreement, a handshake and we were on our way.

It was on to Korea to sell ads for that first issue and back home with a briefcase full of orders. It was the same story with the advertisers in Germany, Holland and Switzerland - two weeks of hard work with an almost 100% acceptance rate. The first issue was a big success and highly accepted. I had found the perfect niche, in the perfect niche market.

From a financial point of view, the business would be primarily billed in US dollars. That was, and still is, the only global currency and it was certainly the currency of the US military market. With the risk of variation in exchange rates, it was in my best interest to have as many costs as possible in US dollars - in other words, dollars in and dollars out. Some of the major costs like sales commissions, printing the Pacific edition in Korea, and distribution costs, could be paid in US dollars but European edition printing and design and reproduction costs would be in UK pounds - so the exchange rate had become a big factor in my life. BBC2 Teletext Page 241 became required viewing.

The higher the value of the US dollar, the lower my costs - hence profit. Any time the pound strengthened, it was, for me, gloom and doom. I never bought forward but simply watched the exchange rate carefully then sold dollars at the most opportune time.

My simple strategy of SELL, SELL, SELL - and keeping the costs LOW, LOW, LOW was paying off handsomely. I negotiated hard with the printers in the U.K. and Korea, shopped around for the lowest-priced airfares and generally ran a very tight operation. Meanwhile, I had bought a new apartment in a central Brighton tower block called Sussex Heights and moved in with Andy and Colin. This was to become our home and my office.

After we had settled in, a typical day would start by Andy leaving early in the morning to catch the train from Brighton to London. I would get up, and check the faxes from Japan and Korea. Then I would run Colin to Longhill School in Rottingdean nearby where we used to live but was now about three miles away. He subsequently moved to BHASVIC College conveniently located in central Brighton. Most of the day was spent doing routine work like phoning Germany and faxing out order confirmations, then cooking a meal for everyone when Andy returned from work. After that, clients in the USA would receive my attention by phone and fax - and then round the day off with a nightcap before retiring.

The divorce was not yet absolute and the house not yet sold, but I at least had my sanity. And I think Andy and Colin had too. By this time, Martin had met the love of his life, Joanne, and they soon moved into their first little love nest.

PARTNERSHIPS ARE BAD NEWS - SO ARE MOST LAWYERS, ACCOUNTANTS AND BANK MANAGERS

Quite by chance, a couple of months before launching 'AVP Special Report', I had bumped into my old Remington colleague, Rod Wheeler, who I hadn't seen for several years. We went for a beer and caught up with our respective lives. He was a talented graphic designer and running a small design studio in his apartment in Sutton - my old hometown. I told him about my plans for 'AVP Special Report' which he thought was a great idea. A sort of partnership was formed. We agreed that I would do the selling and administration while he would take care of the design and layouts etc. We also agreed to put in equal capital and equally share any profits. One problem - he didn't have any money - period. Secondly, despite his lack of specific experience in the military market, he often made decisions without consulting me. That was a recipe for disaster. After getting the first two issues published, I fired him. He didn't like that very much and sued me for damages. The case was kicked out of court two years later. It was the only time in my business career that I used the services of a lawyer.

I really did enjoy working with Rod Wheeler. He was a good friend who helped me through some of the problems related to my divorce. But that's the way it seems to go with partnerships. Apart from a few lawyers and accountants, things never seem to work out too well. So many start full of enthusiasm on the concept that I'm good at this and he is good at that - what a great team we would make. But sooner or later, so many partnerships flounder. It's my opinion that there must be only one ultimate boss.

Two guys who were friends - Len Oliver and David Graimes, started the design and repro firm I used since Rod's departure. One of them got in early, stayed late and would only have a midday sandwich at his desk. The other would arrive late, leave an hour later for a client lunch, and come back after three in the afternoon and then go home early. One claimed he was doing all the work, the other that he was getting all the business. Resentment soon set in. Who was right, I don't know - or even care - but it all ended a few years ago in acrimonious legal battles and the guy who did all the work is now the sole boss. Nowadays, he gets all the business as well as working all hours of the day and often into the night. Oliver & Graimes Design Associates Ltd did a terrific job for 'AVP Special Report' and David Graimes must take all the credit.

In my opinion - always do your own thing - be your own boss and simply buy whatever expertise you may need. Don't be tempted into a partnership.

Obviously, before launching the magazine, I had done my homework and projected figures on both revenues and costs, but I never did a serious formal business plan. I never took advice from the so-called 'professionals' - the lawyers, the accountants or the bank manager. What do they know? I thought. They only trot out the usual platitudes like: "Get everything in the form of a formal, legal contract" or "Never give credit to any organisation without first doing a credit check." Much of the time they seem to be simply creating work for themselves by making things appear as complicated as possible to justify their often extortionate fees. Let them carry out routine duties like bookkeeping or any legal matters that may crop up. But keep them well away from the important functions like selling, marketing and customer service - they simply don't have the necessary experience or know-how. Use them only when you have to but experience, common sense and a supportive spouse are far more important in being successful.

Geoff Davis and his wife Sue, both highly qualified accountants, of Davis & Company, took care of my every detailed need regarding the legal financial requirements of running a U.K. based business. With me being basically a 'one-man-band' and on-the-road for much of the time, Davis & Co did a super job in keeping everything on the straight and narrow with the VAT and TAX men. They constantly chased me for the necessary info that would enable them to get all the returns in on time. I was then able to concentrate on the important things like selling and production while not having to waste time on routine matters like government-inspired form filling. But ask them for advice regarding selling advertising or the quirks of the military market? Forget it - that wasn't their job.

My collection procedures were better than any financial institution could come up with. A simple, faxed 'reminder' followed by a friendly phone call from me always did the trick. My policy was simple: Trust everyone - until they give you some indication that they can't be trusted. If they start to play unfair or be unreasonable - then come down on them hard. Over 15 years, the bad debts were negligible - if you set your calculator to two decimal places, the percentage wouldn't even register. I never invoiced or asked for payment in advance - unless requested by a client who had advertising money to spend and wanted to commit it in this budget period - but always on publication. I never did a single credit check on anyone. From the massive blue-chip companies down to the little guy selling pirate SKY cards to the GIs in Germany, I was never seriously stuffed.

A couple of years after the launch, things changed for me in Japan. Michinori Okada had quit MSJ to form his own media rep company - Tandem Inc. He persuaded Andy Anderson to let him handle *'Overseas'* magazine that left MSJ without a military magazine to represent. Meanwhile, two things happened. Firstly, Tadashi Mori, boss man at MSJ, had promoted a junior salesman, Mikio Tsuchiya, who I knew from the earlier years, to senior salesman to replace Michi. Secondly, Tak Miyagi had been making noises to me that he was getting too tired to pound those Tokyo pavements selling ads preferring to stay in his office carrying out translation and other services.

Lunch with Tad and Mikio established that MSJ would love to handle 'AVP Special Report', so the change was made. Again, no lawyers drawing up expensive contracts - just an agreed summary of who would get what, who would pay for what and handshakes all round were enough. Things went well with MSJ for another couple of years until Mikio decided he too wanted to do his own thing! He called his company MHAS Media - based on the initials of his wife and kids. He pleaded with me, in a very Japanese way, to let him handle the sales of advertising for 'AVP Special Report' in Japan. It was tough shot for me to call because Tad Mori had been my first contact and good friend in Japan where loyalty counts for a great deal. On the other hand, Mikio Tsuchiya understood the military market well and how to sell ads in 'AVP Special Report'. I sent an identical letter to both Tad and Mikio setting out the reasons why I was making the decision I did. It had to be MHAS Media.

I stayed good friends with Tad but became even better friends with Mikio. Not only was I invited to his home several times, a rare enough event for a foreigner in Japan, but, on one occasion, also stayed with the family for several nights. His wife offered absolutely wonderful food and hospitality. And I just loved their teenage daughter and 10-year old son who were fascinated by this European giant (me) in their home. I have to be honest though and say that I would have preferred sleeping in a regular bed, rather than a tatami mat on the floor!

My divorce was finalised with decree absolute issued in August '85, so I was

feeling very happy about that. We had been married 24 years and about 47 weeks - just missing the silver wedding. She had the lion's shares of the spoils, but that was ok with me - at last it was over.

It had been a routine day in the office for me. The commute from my bed to desk had taken its usual ten minutes via the bathroom and there had been a few faxes from Japan during the night. The Spring/Summer 1986 issue of the book was in full distribution all over Europe and the Pacific and

Good friend, Mikio Tsuchiya of MHAS Media, who sold many, many pages of advertising for ' AVP Special Report' in Japan, helping to make the magazine the most successful in the US military markets.

everything had been invoiced. The money was starting to come in and everything was looking good. Later in the day, the phone rang. It was Tom Bowers.

"Hi Derek - just called to let you know there's a new lady in my life."

I gave him the usual bad time, but he really did try to assure me that this time it was different. It had happened like this:

With Tom living in Boston and James living in DC, it was too far for the two friends to meet up too often. But about once every couple of months or so, one of them would fly the shuttle to spend the weekend together. On one trip to DC, Tom had been introduced to the new lady - Isabelle. Of course, since meeting her, he had been travelling down to Washington more frequently.

"Don't waste your hard earned money Tom," I jokingly pleaded.

"But Derek, she's great! You will meet her one day, and then you'll see what I mean."

I did meet her one-day - at Tom's funeral.

A FUNERAL IN YUMA, ARIZONA (1986)

Bob Snyder had called me with the shocking news. Tom was dead at the age of barely 29. He had gone to Washington one Friday evening for a boy's night out with James Kitfield. He then spent all day Saturday with Isabelle. Having gone out for dinner, they spent the night together in Isabelle's flat doing what young lovers always do. They slept but Tom never woke up. I couldn't believe it. I still couldn't believe it when I saw Tom's body lying in the funeral parlour in Yuma, Arizona. At any moment, I thought Tom's eyes would open; he would smile that smile and say, "Fooled ya!" But it wasn't to be - Tom was dead.

Tim Bowers had organised the funeral. He and James compiled a 30-minute cassette of all Tom's favourite music, which was being played at the funeral service as the mourners were arriving. Today, I cannot think of Tom without getting emotional and anytime I hear John Lennon's 'Imagine' or Sinatra and 'New York, New York', I unashamedly cry.

I cry even more when I think of what Tom told me on the phone - "One day you

Talented writer and good friend, James Kitfield. Now living and working in Washington DC writing for a quality defence trade magazine after living for many years in Germany. James was a big help in assisting me getting 'AVP Special Report' off the ground and was a regular contributor throughout.

will meet Isabelle, then you'll see what I mean." Well, I did meet Isabelle and Tom was right. Isabelle was so beautiful, so caring, so understanding and so obviously in love with Tom. They would have been perfect together.

James who wrote and read the eulogy at the service, said what we were all so deeply feeling:

The death of great friend Tom Bowers (bottom right) at just 29 was a massive loss to so many people. But trying to look on the bright side, I have made good friends with all his old pals from Arizona and when we get together, we have great a time. (Clockwise from top) Tim and Norine Bowers and children, Sandy and Vance Riggins, Sanders and Roxy Achen, Michelle, Megan and Dan Mahon

"One of the passions Tom Bowers and I shared, and we shared many, were books. And I remember a comment he would sometimes make after discussing a book we both enjoyed - the last time I heard the comment was this summer in Spain while browsing through a Hemingway exhibit in Pamplona, and reading at what age one of my favorite authors had written this or that book, And Tom would tell me, 'We're waiting on you kid.'

Oh, you can't imagine the effect those hopeful words have on a writer - the perfect mixture of encouragement and prodding. But Tom Bowers knew.

I haven't encountered a lot of tragedy in my life, and I've been stricken over the past few days at how self-centred it can seem. My own mind runs ahead without reign, and I know with a clarity made all the more acute by the sense of loss I feel that there will be gentle encouragements I'll need that no one will know how or when to offer like Tom seemed to know; there will be ironies of life at which I will not be able to laugh because Tom will not be around to make me see them; and there will be other tragedies in my life without anyone I can lean on like I could always lean on Tom Bowers.

But perhaps there is in such selfishness a true measure of the man who was son, brother, lover and friend mourning him, the people who meant most to him in his life. I strongly suspect that for many of you, as for me, there is a feeling that we were never quite so good as when we were around Tom. By his passing we are diminished. And the shadow of grief that we are all under is the more dark, cast as it is by the depth of love he inspired.

I know Tom would have me say this, and we indeed had spoken of it often: though short, his life was remarkably full. He had seen and experienced much, learned from the pain in his life and yet continued to love without reservation. He spoke ill of no one. In short, he was a man who was fine far beyond his years. Tom would also have me say this: that this last year of his life was the happiest, and he took leave of this world in the arms of the woman he loved.

My deepest sympathies go to Isabelle, and to Tom's family: his brother Tim, his sisters Patti and Betsy, and especially his mother Polly. I just hope that you can take some slight consolation in the knowledge that your excruciating grief is commensurate with the love Tom felt for each of you.

Like all of Tom's friends, I had looked forward to sharing my life's journey with him. I understand only now just how much I had counted on that. And knowing Tom will no longer be along those travels tarnishes their allure by a good measure. Still, we have to be grateful, and thank God, for his companionship on the road thus taken. And somewhere, I have to believe that Tom is standing around an unforeseen bend in the road that we all must pass, and mouthing the familiar refrain, 'We're waiting for you kid.'

"The small city of Yuma came to standstill as the local cops held up the traffic to allow the big black limo carrying Tom, followed by hundreds of mourner's cars, to make its way to the burial grounds where Tom was laid to rest together with his dad. To say Polly Bowers was brave would be to use the cliché of the millennium. Her husband had died so young and now her eldest son even younger - from the same rare and difficult to detect heart condition. That day, Polly was a magnificent tower of strength to us all.

As when my parents had died, I tried to find something positive to hang on to about Tom's passing. One big and very positive thing that came out of this tragedy was the great friendships that developed between myself and all Tom's old friends from Arizona - Dan and Michelle, Vance and Sandy, Sanders and Roxy, Bill and Maureen...all great human beings. We usually get together once a year in Phoenix and have a great time. Tim and Norine will come by with the kids, Dan grills steaks and we drink some beer. There's some good music playing in the background and then someone says, "I still miss him you know." "Yeah, me too." And the tears come flooding back...17 years on. Tom was that sort of guy.

THE SECOND TIME AROUND (FROM 1986 FOREVER)

My beautiful wife, Françoise Madeleine, has been so supportive in all my endeavours as well as running her own property business. This photograph was taken on our wedding day in December 1991.

It was shortly after returning from Tom's funeral in November '86, feeling rather sad, that something happened which made me feel a good deal better - I met Françoise. She was to be a breath of fresh air in my life. She had a magic sparkle in her eyes that I found hard to resist - and I really didn't try that hard to resist. It was like that. On our first evening out at the 'Plough' in Rottingdean she told me her story:

She was born Françoise Madeleine Lefevre during the second world war in St Cyr en Pail, Normandy, France. After her mother had died when she was four, her father didn't really want to know, so she was brought up by her aunty and uncle, Annette and Alfred Lefevre in Falaise - William the Conqueror's birthplace. Spending most of the early years at boarding school, she came to England in 1958 at the age of 17 as an au pair to improve her english. Françoise never went back to France - apart from holidays that is.

For a while, she worked with one family as a genuine 'au pair' but soon moved to another couple without children. This time more as a general help around the home and with their business. Françoise joined up with William Edgar and Ella Louisa Phillips who lived in a good-sized house in Woodland Drive, Hove. 'Phil', as his friends called him, ran an estate agency and a number of small property companies that had developed the Mile Oak area of Portslade; while Ella was one of the old fashioned type of wives. She didn't get directly involved in the business but ran the home on a full time basis and supported her husband in every way possible.

The Phillips could not, for whatever reason, have children of their own. They both loved Françoise dearly and regarded her as their own daughter. In fact, that is what she became - their daughter. They legally adopted Françoise at the age of 20. She then became Françoise Madeleine Phillips and British.

Françoise loved it! She had recognised the opportunity of a stable life, with a mum and dad, after being in and out of boarding schools for so many years. She embraced it all with the passion and intense energy of a true French person. She worked in the family business for several years before falling in love and marrying a Mr Peter Rumball. A year later, they had twin boys, Richard and Julian, and life was set fair. It was, for several years, but, like so many marriages these days, it went wrong. Divorce finally followed in 1985 - coincidentally, just about the time as my own divorce was being finalised.

Françoise fascinated me and we saw more and more of each other over the following months. Unlike my own divorce, Françoise's was relatively quick and easy. They had negotiated their own split without too much 'help' from solicitors. There were enough funds available for each to buy their own house and Françoise had purchased an attractive one in Marine Avenue, Hove. What impressed me about her was that, unlike so many women I had known, she would think and plan ahead. Unsure of her future financial circumstances, her new home had not only enough room for herself and the twins, but also a separate self-contained one bedroom flat. She reasoned that if things got tough, she could always rent out the flat.

Incidentally, other things to impress me about Françoise in the early days were that she could read a map and give directions. Also, when we were out together and had to use the little boys and little girl's room, she would always be quicker than me! Up to that moment in my life, I had never known a woman who had a sense of direction or could powder her nose in anything less 20 minutes!

Françoise and myself entertaining Grandma Phillips and old school friends, Arthur and Glenda James in the garden of our Saltdean, Brighton home. The 'shed' in the background was my office and saved me a tremendous amount of rent. That boosted profits and helped us make a great deal of money.

WORKING IN THE 'SHED' (1988 - 2000)

After two years, we loved and trusted each other completely. We pooled our resources and moved in together. We agreed to sell both her house and my flat to buy our own love nest. She quickly sold Marine Avenue at a decent profit but my flat stuck for a while. Long enough to hit the property slump of the late 80s. Luckily, we found a suitable affordable house for our new 5-piece family by adding some capital to the proceeds of Françoise's sale and not needing the money from the sale of my flat. Instead, we rented out the flat in Sussex Heights, which supplemented our income very nicely.

Martin and Jo were already married and settled in their victorian flat in Blackheath, SE London while Andy was house hunting for herself. What we needed was a place for us two lovebirds, and our remaining children Colin, Richard and Julian. A house in Bishopstone Drive, Saltdean, proved perfect.

On the business side of things, 'AVP Special Report' was doing very well in 1988. Françoise was a huge motivator for me. When I said I would be going on a business trip, she wouldn't whinge about having to stay at home and eating peanut butter sandwiches. She would simply ask, "How many clean shirts will you need?" You don't know what a big difference an attitude like that made. When I closed a big a deal, Françoise got as big a buzz as I did.

Often I would get a call from clients who were visiting England. We always invited them to stay with us for the night or a couple of nights. Françoise would prepare a lovely meal with a bottle or two of burgundy, and we would have a very enjoyable evening. I never asked her to do this - she would suggest it, as she knew it would help in my endeavours. That level of support was superb. But simply not having her complain would have been enough for me.

Françoise had herself taken over the running of the property companies since her Dad died earlier in the year. While not getting directly involved in her business, I would obviously talk over any problems with her and would give her the benefit of a common sense viewpoint if not exactly a fully informed property person's opinion.

For the first time in my life I had a true partner in every sense of the word - lover, friend and business confidant. Not just someone who was there simply using me for their own selfish needs and not making any real contribution to the relationship - either financially or with any sort of moral support.

We legalised our commitment in 1991 by getting married in Hove Registry Office. Neither of us really felt the need to make it legal but we thought it would be a great excuse for a party. And what a party we had! The Norfolk Hotel on Brighton's seafront that night swung to the fabulous voice of american jazz singer, Joe Lee Wilson, supported by a knockout band of some of the best musicians in Brighton - Norman Evans on tenor sax, Peter Gold on drums, Bob Mitchell on piano and Dave Edwards on bass. The interval band was even better! Derek Halling on trumpet, Norman Garner on tenor, Terry Clark on piano... seriously though, we played reasonably well and certainly had a great time reviving all the memories of those early gigs back in our school days. Françoise and myself asked that no one should give wedding presents but make a contribution to a far more deserving cause - 'Children in Need'. Over £1000 was collected. We honeymooned by travelling first-class around the world via the States, Hawaii, Japan and Malaysia. We returned home feeling just wonderful.

The great thing was that we could be happy with a totally clear conscience. Despite our unhappy first marriages, we stood by our respective children until they were old enough to almost make their own ways in the world. We had done our duty - that rather strange old-fashioned word which, today, fewer and fewer people seem to know the meaning. So many mothers and fathers are shirking the responsibility for their children by leaving them to the other partner. Many don't see their kids for years sometimes after which remorse sets in. On realising their own selfishness, they then wonder, when they do try to re-establish a relationship, why their own flesh and blood doesn't really want to know them any more.

It would be nice if my three kids appreciate what I did for them, but I am not really that bothered. All I care about is that neither Martin, Andy nor Colin can ever point a finger at me and say, "Where were you, dad, when I needed you?"

Andy, having met Mr Right the previous year, also married in 1991. Her man was Michael John Heaton, a salesman for Allied Domecq - the wines and spirits people. Having a daughter and now a son-in-law in the booze business was a real bonus! One major problem however - I have not been able to sell him on the idea of becoming a Seagulls fan. Wolverhampton who?

Françoise's mum died in 1995 at the ripe old age of almost 91. She was the last of the nice old-fashioned ladies in my life. My own Mother would have been the same age as her - had she not died those 32 years earlier. I do sometimes wonder how the two ladies would have got on.

In the later years of her life, Grandma Phillips was in need of constant care and attention, so money played a very important part in being able to provide it. That taught me another important lesson. To grow old and grey without a couple of quid in your pocket (or handbag) is a depressing thought. It certainly made Françoise and myself be sure to have enough tucked under the mattress, in case either or both of us should be lucky enough to reach our nineties and find either of us in the same situation.

Back to 1988. In a determination to keep costs to an absolute minimum, I continued to work from home. I could have had a room in the new house but with two 19 year olds and an 18-year old's music to contend with, I thought it better if I could have a separate work environment. The answer was the 'Shed', to be built in the back garden. It wasn't to be any old shed mind you. It was 20 X 10 feet, decently built in timber to the same specs as wooden houses are built in New Zealand. It was fitted out with power, three telephone lines, photocopier, fax machine, computers and most other modern conveniences except running water. That meant a 10 pace trip back into the house for Ts and Ps! Such a hard life...!

It cost us just £1200 to have the 'Shed' built in 1988 and it is still in perfect order in 2004. That is a rental equivalent of under £100 PA or less than £2 per week! That's what keeping costs down really means!"

LOCATION, LOCATION, LOCATION - NOT

When I was splitting with Andy Anderson, he held the opinion that it would be impossible to run a U.S. military magazine from England. To him it had to be Germany or the U.S.A. I was delighted to prove him wrong.

Andy Anderson was locked into the old philosophy that you had to be based in a credible location to succeed. I would agree with that opinion when talking about retail stores but for most other types of businesses, it really doesn't matter. Anderson would say you needed the right sort of prestigious, or at least semi-prestigious, address to be successful. That people would simply not do business with you if you were in the wrong part of town. Just like the U.K. newspaper industry in the old days - you had to be in Fleet Street. Well, Eddie Shah broke that mould - like so many other moulds have since been broken. All sorts of businesses have relocated in less prestigious, less expensive areas and their revenues have not dropped one penny while their costs have. 'Thinking' clients don't give a damn where your business is located as long as you give them the service and attention they require.

Over the years, I have never expected my clients to have to contact me - I would always contact them. On the other hand, I have never 'hassled' any of my clients by sitting on their doorstep or constantly phoning them unnecessarily. I have always assessed the level of attention they appear to like and give it to them. Any complaints or if anything ever went wrong, I would be on the next plane to put out the fire. That's what customers liked, so that's what I gave them. Did they care that I was operating out of the 'Shed' in Saltdean? Of course not.

OPERATING IN A DECLINING MARKET (1995-2000)

'AVP Special Report' was to become the most successful surviving military market magazine of the '90s. With the Iron Curtain coming down in 1989 and the subsequent end of the cold war, drawdowns had become the order the day. The total number of American forces stationed in Europe had dropped by two thirds since the post war peak. This had meant a big reduction in sales revenues for both the PXs and the manufacturers. The rep companies have suffered badly, too. Many have gone out of business, but the toughest still survive - mainly by 'stealing' lines from other rep companies.

To make matters worse from an advertising point of view, 'Stars & Stripes' newspaper had been authorised by Congress to sell advertising space to commercial as well as military organizations. That was an extra nail in the coffin for some of the independent magazines.

The reduction in military activity had actually benefited 'AVP Special Report'. As the overall level of business had gone down, all manufacturers reviewed their strategies. Fewer area reps, fewer instore demonstrators, cut backs on travel expenses, and a review of advertising budgets which invariably meant less. With less money to spend, manufacturers had been basically asking the question, "Where do I get the biggest bang for my buck?" Ninety nine percent of the time the answer came back - 'AVP Special Report'. And that suited me just fine. Pages would be cut from the ad schedules from expensive magazines with high overheads - like 'Off Duty' and I would get more. Equal quality, more precise targeting and much cheaper. I could also offer low ad rates - after all, I was only paying £2 a week office rent!

The ad revenue income kept steady and after paying all the design, print and distribution bills, there were always some nickels and dimes left over to throw into the pot for that proverbial rainy day. Françoise would also throw in her loose change, so we managed to buy a retail shop and add yet another flat to our investment portfolio. I made myself a rule after I had saved the £100 while in the army, that no matter how little or much money I earned over the years, I would always save a reasonable proportion. Earn £3, spend £1 on necessities, £1 on good times and save £1 - that's the way to do it. Françoise has the same attitude. Together we have found what I believe is the right balance between having a good time now and thinking about that rainy day. And, believe me, that rainy day will always come.

Meanwhile, the military magazines were falling one by one. 'Shoppers BiWeekly News' was absorbed by 'R&R', which was followed by the death of my old magazine, 'Overseas'. There was a great deal of personal sweat and blood in that one, but somehow I didn't feel too much pain. Next to go was Robert Beltz' 'AFN TV Guide' followed by 'O'Seas Post'. It was published by a good old friend of mine, Shakeeb 'Jack' Juratli, more commonly known as 'Jack the Rat', but actually one of the nicest guys in the market. The last I heard, Jack was importing socks

The Halling Clan at a get together in 1998.

First born son, Martin with his lovely wife Joanne.

Daughter Andrea (or Andy to just about everyone) with her husband Michael John.

Second son Colin.

Grandson, James together with one of the Seagulls heroes, Rod Thomas, at the Withdean Stadium - Brighton & Hove Albion's new temporary ground.

Stepson twins Richard (left) and Julian Rumball.

The two most beautiful grand daughters in the world! Alexandra Kate(left, daughter of Andy and Mike) and Victoria Elizabeth (Martin and Joanne's daughter)- taken in 1999.

Brother Trevor with his wife Loretta. Trevor and myself have taken very different paths through our lives but he has always been a big influence on me and helped me to form many of my basic philosophies.

and towels from Syria and Italy and selling them on the German domestic market. *'Off Duty'* disappeared but *'R&R'* still manages to just about hang in there under Andy Anderson who is now well into his eighties.

So in 1999, it was *'AVP Special Report'* getting most of the image and other high quality advertising while *'Stars & Stripes'* mopped up all the promotional '$10 off - buy it today' type ads. The total advertising spend had dropped by millions of dollars since the boom days of the late '70s and '80s. The market was declining, but surviving. Bouncing along the bottom you might say, but it was tired, very tired. Maybe it was time for me to make a change, and consider 'retirement' by giving up the magazine.

NO MORE RESPONSIBILITIES (2000)

With the arrival of a new Millennium, Françoise and myself decided to review our situation and future. With all the children well and truly off hand and successful in what they are doing with their lives, we have no more responsibilities in that department. Martin and Joanne had been married for 15 years. James William, our oldest grandchild, was born in 1989 followed by Victoria 'Tori' Elizabeth in 1992. Martin and Jo both have good careers and seem to have the same attitude as me. That is: generate the wealth first then decide how to spend it. Not like so many people today who want it now and will borrow to get it now and run up massive debts before getting into trouble when they get the sack.

Since the birth of their daughter Alexandra 'Ali' Kate in 1992, Andy and Michael John decided that Andy would be a full time wife and mother. Andy's departure from the workplace was a great loss to the world of professional selling. She was one of the best. Mike's not a bad salesman either but since his climb up the Allied Domecq corporate ladder, he is now several strata removed from the coalface. However, he still has to regularly use his professional salesman's skills he honed while on-the-road.

Richard took quite a while to know which direction he wanted to go but has also become a salesman of fine distinction. He runs his own taxi business and develops property at the same time. His aim is to be financially independent in seven years time - when he is forty. Julian on the other hand, sells commercial property based in west London. He earns a basic salary plus a healthy commission on every deal that he closes.

Colin is the creative one in our family. He joined his uncle Trevor, my brother, and his cousin Nicholas, Trevor's son, in the world of journalism. Trevor and Nick both work in television while Colin is a managing editor for the Platts Division of the McGraw Hill newsgathering organisation. They report on world commodities and publish daily newsletters and other communications for their worldwide list of subscribers.

Neither Colin, Richard nor Julian has yet found Ms. Right. When they do, I only hope they don't get blinded like I did all those years ago by choosing someone with all the good looks but lacking any sense of the sometimes hard, realistic aspects of life.

The main reality is that survival is the strongest of man's instincts. And just to survive in the modern world you need a few necessities - a home, warmth and food - and they cost money. If the whole family agrees it wants more than the basics - new cars every year, wine with every meal, fashionable new clothes and jewellery, frequent holidays, eating out in smart restaurants and private education for the children - then the family needs more money. And that has to be earned.

One could rob a bank, win the lottery or scrounge off rich relatives, but for most of us ordinary people, one has to work for someone else or run your own business. To earn more, the breadwinner needs to work harder and that probably means longer hours. Longer hours mean less time with the family - and that is a price that has to be paid.

Whoever earns the money in a relationship - one or the other, or both - needs support, both physical and moral. You cannot do an effective money making job

Gerry Haine, at our regular New Years Eve party on 31st December 1999, surrounded by 'Les Girls' of the Cranleigh crowd. From left to right: Barbara Haine, Kath Stebbings, Brenda Jervis, Jan McCall, Françoise Halling, and Maureen Turner. Founder member and chief laughter raiser, Betty Mader, *(inset)* was struck down by a bug and unfortunately missed one hell of a party. Special millennium t-shirts were the order of the party and worn by *(left to right)* Peter Turner, Basil Jervis, Alan McCall and myself..

with a feeling that your partner just doesn't care. If you are constantly worrying that your spouse is wasting too much money on buying unnecessary new things behind your back or even siphoning money from your joint account into their own private account, then you've got major problems. And your job performance - hence your moneymaking potential - will suffer.

ROGUES AND PRO SALESMEN

Françoise and myself have travelled extensively during the past sixteen years - much of it on business but increasingly for pleasure. We have stayed in the smartest hotels, sailed on the finest cruise ships and generally enjoyed the best of all good things. One big decision made all this possible - becoming a salesman on 14 February 1959. Selling did it for me. Selling has been a way of life that has given me not only the material benefits but also so much satisfaction. I can honestly say that I have never lied or cheated or pushed anyone into buying something for which they did not have a genuine need. Ask any professional salesman, and he or she will tell you the same thing.

The media always highlight the 'rogues' - those salesmen who rip-off a pensioner of their few hundred quid life savings for double-glazing they didn't really need. Or the Arthur Daley type - second-hand car salesman who fitted someone up with a dodgy motor. You never hear about the 'pros' - those highly skilful honest salesmen who do a damn good job for their clients day-in and day-out. Take Gerry Haine, one of the Cranleigh crowd, for example. He sold postage and other high value stamps for Harrisons the Printers for over 40 years - mainly export. He personally generated millions of pounds worth of business from a whole variety of countries from Saudi Arabia to Kenya adding tremendously to the wealth of himself, his firm and his country.

Others in the Cranleigh crowd are also great pro salesmen. Alan McCall is probably one of the UKs most knowledgeable plastic extrusion machinery salesmen and Basil Jervis has been selling electrical metal enclosures for more years than he cares to remember. Peter Turner, on the other hand, is one of those clever salesmen who knows just about everything there is to know about electronics and computers. All of these guys have carved out wonderful lifestyles for themselves and their families - and all because they are great professional salesmen. But professional salesmen just aren't news I'm afraid. It's only the rogues who hit the headlines. But never mind that, selling is a profession of which to be truly proud.

So did I come to any conclusions when I was sipping my gin and tonic in Cape Town back in '96? Was it all luck? Well, being in the right place at the right time helps but is certainly not everything. Fate? I guess it was fate that I was born in relatively prosperous southeast England. That gave me a real head start over all those born in one of those shantytown homesteads we passed in the Rolls Royce in Cape Town

All my own doing? Mostly, I must say. Without a determination to succeed, nothing happens in this world. You can't sit around waiting for someone to give you a hand out. If you really want something or be someone, then you have to make it happen yourself.

If you have previously read many career or management books, you will have noticed how they tell you to set goals and then plan the necessary steps to enable you to achieve that goal. You know the sort of thing:

"So you wanna be President of the USA by the time you are 35? No problem. First step - go to college. Second step - become a lawyer. Third step - become a Senator or Congressman by the age of 25" and so on. For some, that may be just fine. But for most of us ordinary people, it usually doesn't work like that. How many of us know what we want to do in our careers at, say, the age 18 or even 20? Not many of us, I would suggest. Most find ourselves in circumstances probably created by our parents and we simply don't have a clue where our future lies. It is only when some sort of opportunity is presented to the individual, like seeing a 'situations vacant' ad in a newspaper or talking to a careers officer, that something sparks. The real skill in life is being able to recognise those opportunities and evaluate them. You must grab one, then put every ounce of your energy and determination into making it work.

SELLING IN ITS BROADEST SENSE

Whichever path life takes, the word 'selling', in its broadest sense, is tremendously important. Communicating and influencing others to your way of thinking enters every aspect of your life. Preparing your CV and covering letter in an attention getting way and presenting yourself well and what you have to offer at job interviews is all selling. You also have to sell yourself to your boss for getting that promotion or getting a pay rise. Don't just sit around waiting for it to happen - sell the idea to someone.

For the past few years, everyone thought they could become an instant millionaire by doing something on the Internet or floating a dot.com company. In my opinion, that was very wishful thinking unless you had paid careful attention to selling. You needed financial backing? Then that venture capitalist or bank manager needed selling on your particular proposition to make it stand out from the hundreds of proposals they get every day. And what good is a website unless everyone knows it exists? Enough people must be 'sold' on finding your site from the literally millions of others that are available on the web. Despite the enormous growth in e-activity today, just being there is not enough. Enormous advertising budgets have been spent on TV and in the print media simply to sell us consumers on visiting their particular website to raise the level of 'hits' so that their site becomes attractive to potential sponsors or advertisers. Remember, without someone somewhere selling somebody something, nothing happens in this world.